UPGRADE YOUR LIFE

Books by the Speakmans

Conquering Anxiety

Winning at Weight Loss

Everyday Confidence

UPGRADE YOUR LIFE

*Break your unconscious barriers
and live the life you deserve*

NIK & EVA
SPEAKMAN

First published in Great Britain in 2022 by Orion Spring
an imprint of The Orion Publishing Group Ltd
Carmelite House, 50 Victoria Embankment
London EC4Y 0DZ

An Hachette UK Company

1 3 5 7 9 10 8 6 4 2

A CIP catalogue record for this book is available from the British Library.

ISBN (Trade Paperback) 978 1 8418 8327 4
ISBN (eBook) 978 1 8418 8328 1
ISBN (Audio) 978 1 4091 9258 9

Printed in Great Britain by Clays Ltd, Elcograf, S.p.A

MIX
Paper from
responsible sources
FSC® C104740

www.orionbooks.co.uk

ORION
SPRING

In Memory of Grandad George

Important Information
Before Reading this Book

This book is not a substitute for medical or psychological intervention, nor is the content intended to replace therapy, or medical help and advice.

While we are confident that this book will help to positively alter your perspective and attitude in relation to your confidence and yourself, there are no guarantees. If you feel that your lack of confidence is detrimentally affecting your mental health, or is contributing to your anxiety or psychological wellbeing, we would recommend speaking to your GP.

We would also always strongly encourage you to speak with your doctor or health professional about how you are feeling, and also to enquire about therapy should you feel that this is necessary or that you need emotional help and support.

Contents

Introduction

Deep inside, everyone knows the person they would love to be and the life they would love to live, yet there often appear to be invisible barriers preventing them from living that life. Does that sound familiar to you? Perhaps you have a very clear vision of the person you want to become, but you struggle with how to get there. If the barriers between us and our future selves are invisible, then how do we begin to tackle them and upgrade to the lives we dream of? Well, it's not just you. We have been just where you are, and we learned to remove our own invisible barriers to create lives full of joy and purpose. And we did it with the simple tools in this book, which will allow anyone – yes, even you – to live the life you deserve.

It is often said that 'simplicity is genius', and we fully agree, which is why we're not going to overcomplicate this book. We know how off-putting a very long book can be when you're busy (and let's face it, who isn't?), so we intend to keep this as simple, effective and, most of all, life-changing as possible. You won't have to read through pages of waffle in order to get to the point where you discover how you can make changes in your life. We're going to get straight into it!

We really don't want you to have to do any more work than is absolutely necessary. That is why we've made this amazing process of change as straightforward as possible, so you can get on with the important job of making yourself happier, feeling more fulfilled and allowing your life to flow more easily.

But let's not pretend that there is no work involved on your part. If you want to upgrade your life, you're going to need to put in a bit of effort. If you were upgrading your phone, you'd do some research, shop around, talk to friends, check out deals – let's do the same to upgrade our lives, which is a far more important and lasting process. Just to be clear, we are not talking hard manual labour here, just absorbing new information and putting it into practice. Anything worth having is worth working for, and without doubt you are, and always will be, the best project that you will ever work on.

Let us give you an example. At the age of twenty, Nik decided to set a goal to read a new book on psychology and self-improvement every week, and he's continued this practice to this day. While he has learned a huge amount from the wisdom and experience of these authors, the biggest lesson has been that reading only gets you so far. If you want to make changes in your life, you have to put your learning into action. You are the only person who knows what you want from your life, so it is only you who can make those things happen.

We like to think of the tools we are about to share with you as a baton in a relay race. Right now, we have the tools you need, and we're going to hand them to you – and then it's up to you to run with them. The more you practise with these tools, the easier they become, until, like they are for us, they are just a part of the way you live your life too.

Like any great achievement in life, there are tasks we have to complete to make them happen. To allow you to obtain maximum benefit from this book, for your great achievement at upgrading your life, we have added tasks and exercises at the end of each chapter.

Structure, organisation and repetition are key in creating habits, and therefore we would recommend using a diary to jot down your daily tasks. This is why we have shared affirmations with you too.

Say your affirmations when you wake in the morning and before you go to bed. You can say them at lunchtime and during the day too if you are able. Repeat each affirmation five to ten times. Listen to yourself saying them, focusing on the words as they leave your mouth. As you say each affirmation, really feel them and believe them to be true.

We always lead by example, so we're not teaching you anything that we haven't tried, tested and succeeded with ourselves. We know these tools work as they have brought immense happiness and fulfilment not only into our lives, but also into those of the many people we have shared them with over the years in our private practice, our workshops and our events.

We're excited to get you started in creating your most fulfilled and happy life!

Your Personal-Life Upgrade

Before you continue reading about how to upgrade your life, we would like you to consider what your own personal upgrade looks like. Only you will know the parts of your life that you would like to change the most; no one else can do that for you. Knowing what you want your life to look like is the first step to creating it. Having clarity about your future self, and a clear vision to aim for, will help you shape your upgraded life.

Have you ever considered how absolutely everything that surrounds you on a day-to-day basis, with the exception of nature, started as a thought in someone's mind? Just knowing this alone will help you realise how powerful your thoughts are. Take a look around you, wherever you are – that chair, that painting, the buildings you can see, the curtains at the window all started as a simple thought, which became reality. To turn a thought into reality is an incredible power, and we all possess it! This is why it's so important for you to start to think about the life you would like and everything that you would like in it too. At first, many people struggle to think of what they want, so please don't worry if that's you. It may help if you consider this: if you woke up tomorrow and everything in your life was entirely perfect, what would it look like?

We often settle, adapt, make do or just go with the flow as opposed to being true to ourselves and asking ourselves what we truly desire. We tell ourselves to be realistic, rather than to reach for the stars. But in this case we positively encourage you to reach for the stars – and the sun and the moon too! Not everything you dream of may be attainable or possible immediately, but your vision is the starting point, and you must not at this stage allow ability, age, marital status, financial status, qualifications or responsibilities to be a barrier. So, if you want a beach house in Miami, for example, don't tell yourself you'll never afford it – let yourself imagine everything you hope for. There are many people in the world who have and continue to achieve the most amazing things and you really are no different to them. If you can see it in your mind, you can make it happen.

There is no greater project to work on than yourself, and we would now like you to sit somewhere quiet, with no distractions, while you consider the answers to the questions that follow, using the mindset that your answers are based upon a world where you have no barriers whatsoever. If you need more space for your responses, feel free to use a journal for your answers instead.

If anything were possible . . .

Work

WHAT CAREER WOULD YOU HAVE? WHAT WORK
POSITION WOULD YOU BE IN? WOULD YOU BE
EMPLOYED/SELF-EMPLOYED? RETIRED?

*Working as a therapist maybe 3
days a week and understaking
more psychological based training*

Home

WHAT KIND OF HOUSE WOULD YOU LIVE IN?

*3/4 detatched/Semi detatched
with a nice sized garden, a gerage
a drive and a loft bedroom*

Transport

WHAT CAR OR CARS WOULD YOU BE DRIVING? OR
PERHAPS YOU DREAM OF A MOTORBIKE, HELICOPTER OR
OTHER MODE OF TRANSPORT?

Golf GTE

Friendships

WHO WOULD YOUR FRIENDS BE/WHAT KIND OF FRIENDS
WOULD YOU HAVE? WHAT KIND OF FRIEND WOULD YOU
BE?

Friends would be those who add
value to my life and aren't a
chore to be around. I would be
a reliable friend who made
people feel their best when I'm
around.

Leisure

WHAT KIND OF HOBBIES WOULD YOU HAVE?

- Rock Climbing
- Drawing
- Hiking
- Football

Appearance

WHAT WOULD YOU LOOK LIKE? (For example: size, weight, body tone, heavier, lighter, long hair, short hair, etc.)

- Toned body - fitting into Small + short
- Short hair but not too short. Over my forehead and thick from my transplant

Relationship

WHAT KIND OF A RELATIONSHIP WOULD YOU BE IN?
WHO WOULD YOUR PERECT PARTNER BE? WHAT KIND OF
PARTNER WOULD YOU BE?

One full of trust. They would be my best friend. They'd be funny, have the kindest heart, handsome and someone I would want to raise a family with.

Travel

WHAT COUNTRIES WOULD YOU HAVE VISITED? WHAT
EXPERIENCES WOULD YOU HAVE TRIED? (e.g. scuba
diving, zip lining, ice skating, hot-air ballooning, flying an
aircraft, going on a cruise, swimming with sharks, etc.)

Canada, Italy, Australia, Cyprus
Florida.

Fast car driving

Personality

WHAT PERSONALITY TRAITS WOULD YOU HAVE/NOT
HAVE? (e.g. confident, funny, happy, no anxiety, grateful,
bubbly, etc.)

· Confident · Happy · Kind

· Not depressed, · Grateful

· Content

Achievements

WHAT THINGS WOULD YOU HAVE ACHIEVED? (e.g.
passed an exam, done charity work, gained qualifications,
got married, had children, got pets, bought a home, ran a
marathon, written a book.)

· Become a therapist

· Married, 1 child

· Dog

· Ran marathon

Now that you have built a clear picture of what the perfect life looks like to you, keep hold of this and refer back to it often to remind yourself of the vision you have created.

Life Upgrade

When new smartphones hit the market, people always scramble to be the first to own the latest version, and when upgrades of operating systems are released we all upgrade to the newest and latest software so that our phones are fully up to date and we are able to freely access new and exciting apps and programs. Upgrades also get rid of bugs and glitches in operating systems, allowing our phones to run more smoothly and not slow down. Just as we upgrade our technology, it's essential to be aware of our thoughts and feelings so that we can regularly upgrade those too. It's important to consider any thought processes, feelings and beliefs that do not serve us well, so that we can challenge and de-glitch them, to positively develop our emotions and allow ourselves to be the best that we can be.

The next exercise asks you to take time right now to consider how many of your behaviours are no longer needed in your life or might even be holding you back. For so many of us these unhelpful, or even destructive, behaviours come from older operating systems and ideas we had when we were younger. Well, just like your phone, it's time to upgrade your current operating system to give you the life you just outlined above.

We would now like you to take a moment to consider behaviours that you no longer need, you don't like or that do not serve you and record them in the table opposite.

Behaviour/ belief you no longer need	Who or what event may have created this?	Why is this person or event no longer relevant to you today? Why should you not continue to take advice from them?	What positive beliefs or thoughts can you take from this and why?
Example: Jealousy or anger towards someone, low self-esteem, thinking the worst, being anxious, social anxiety, etc.	Example: Schoolfriends teasing me about my appearance.	Example: I don't even know these people anymore, and I look different now I've grown up.	Example: We were all young. It wasn't personal to me, as they were like that to many others, etc.
Isolating from People who love me	being bullied in School So isolating myself	These people are nothing to do with me now	People who love me are not going to hurt me They choose to be around me
Having to do everything myself. Not trusting people to help	Transitioning young and having to do things by myself	I am not 14 anymore and people want to help	I don't have to worry about being too young to make choices I'm an adult now

(Table continued overleaf)

(Table continued)

Behaviour/ belief you no longer need	Who or what event may have created this?	Why is this person or event no longer relevant to you today? Why should you not continue to take advice from them?	What positive beliefs or thoughts can you take from this and why?
That I have to be perfect or it's not worth doing	Teachers and family having high standards of me	I am not in school anymore. Nobody can live to perfection	Grey exists and I need to be okay with middle
Using drugs to numb my feelings	Feeling heartbroken by Ian, they would make me less anxious	Ian is not in my life. I don't have to worry about him. I am living without him	I didn't think I could live without him but now my life is better. I'm not in a constant state of anxiety

Now you have a clear idea not just of what your perfect life might look like, but what some of the obstacles might be to achieving this dream. We ask you to be as honest as possible with yourself in identifying the behaviours you want to let go of, as we are about to share with you our tools for overcoming these obstacles. We can't release something we haven't admitted to – so don't hold back.

Getting to Know You

No one is born with an opinion of themselves. Our opinions are shaped by our environment and our life experiences. This often means that, by the time we reach adulthood, the way we see ourselves is based on how other people have made us feel.

For example, your children, a partner, parent or friend may have made you feel you are a loving and kind person, yet a school bully, abusive partner, parent, sibling or unkind teacher at school may have made you feel worthless.

We would therefore now like you to list in the table overleaf all the *positive* opinions you have about yourself or traits that you see in yourself, and note anyone significant who may have contributed to you feeling that way.

Positive opinions about yourself or positive traits you have	Who may have contributed to you feeling like this? Be exact. Write their name. Could it have been a parent, grandparent, sister, brother, partner, friend, teacher, employer, etc.?
Examples: Kind, ambitious, fun, honest, beautiful, patient, intelligent, a good listener, helpful, great cook, fair, etc.	
Smart	Parents, Nan, boys School
Thoughtful	family, friends
Spontaneous	family, friends

From this exercise, you have now created a list not only of your own positive traits, but of positive people who you should endeavour to be around, listen to and ask advice from if you ever need it. Even if those people are no longer here, you should make a decision today to remember what they said when they were with you.

It is important that you acknowledge these people, what they said and how they made you feel, as positive feedback is never given without reason. A compliment is a gift, and not to listen to these words would be no different to rejecting any other wonderful gift obtained especially for you. To reject this gift would be unkind and hurtful to the bearer.

We would now like you to repeat this process, noting any negative opinions you may have about yourself or negative traits you see in yourself in the table overleaf.

Negative opinions about yourself or negative traits you have	Who may have contributed to you feeling like this? Be exact and write down their names
Examples: Shy, ugly, useless, negative, etc.	
fat	myself, bullies
Selfish	School bullies, Michael
Not wanted	Potential love interests
Paranoid	Ian

From this exercise, you now have a list of negative traits and also people who you should avoid or distance yourself from, and whose reasons for being unkind to you, such as jealousy perhaps, you should question.

As you read through this book, you will realise that any people who have ever put you down or made you feel bad about yourself have usually done so because they in turn feel bad about themselves. Perhaps they are jealous of you, or afraid of losing you, and therefore by making you feel bad, they hope to clip your wings to stop you flying away. Another frequent reason for people being unkind is that they have learned this behaviour from their own home environment or that they themselves have low self-esteem, and therefore they pull you down to elevate their status. It is so important to understand that their behaviour is about them, and not about you, so don't take it personally even if it was hurtful at the time.

In the table overleaf, we would now like you to note a person who made you feel bad about yourself and consider the reasons why what they said to you was untrue. Maybe they were jealous or didn't really know you, maybe they or you misunderstood the situation, perhaps it was said in the heat of the moment, they were too inexperienced to justify what they were saying or they came from a toxic situation themselves, etc.

Person who made you feel bad about yourself	You should not listen to this person's opinion because . . .
Ian	He is a liar and lives his life full of secrets
Bullies. Michael Mrs D'amato	They are not part of my life now.
Gerard.	He is only Temporary in my life
Myself	I can't trust myself

You should now have a much better understanding of the obstacles and belief systems that stand between you and the dream life you have imagined. With this new clarity, we're ready to move on to the tools that will help you push past these blocks – LET'S GO!

The Speakmans' Schema Conditioning Psychotherapy®

We're excited to introduce you to a powerful set of tools, which we have used to transform our own lives, and which we know will help change yours for the better. We have developed Schema Conditioning Psychotherapy®, which directly tackles our mistaken beliefs about ourselves, challenges them and ultimately allows us to let them go.

So, you might be wondering, what is a schema? The simplest explanation is that a schema is an automatic and often unconscious reference for how we think and act. Schemas are habitual behaviours that are repeated again and again and, as the eminent psychologist Jean Piaget says, 'governed by a core meaning'.

What does that mean exactly? We like to use an old type of analogy, comparing schemas to files within a filing cabinet in your brain. Each file (or schema) instructs us on how to react when we receive incoming stimuli or information. Schemas are a 'learned reference' that allow us to be proficient in everything we do, from brushing our teeth to driving our car to how we communicate. Our brain recognises the pattern and takes out the existing file, and you react to the stimulus in the same way you have reacted before.

For example, we all have schemas for eating out in a restaurant. The schema will be stored with a pattern that includes looking at the menu, choosing food, ordering food, eating and then paying the bill. Whenever you are in a restaurant you will unconsciously run this schema and react accordingly. You may have realised that when you read a menu, for example, your schemas are triggered and as you look through the menu you can sometimes taste the food before you order.

Everything you learn creates a schema or reference (similar to a software program on a computer), which goes into a database within your brain. Your brain then stores this reference or schema, and will use it for specific acts, behaviours and reactions, whether good or bad, until such time as you condition or change that behavioural schema by receiving new information or evidence to update it.

We are all born with a small number of innate schemas. For example, babies have a sucking reflex, which is triggered by something touching a baby's lips. Similarly, when something touches a baby's hand the grasping reflex is elicited. The majority of schemas, however, are learned. They are learned as a result of copying the behaviour of our parents or people we're in close contact with, or through personal life experiences and our individual interpretation of those experiences.

It's for this reason that we all see the world differently, and why you may see someone's behaviour as 'irrational' or 'brave' compared to how you would react in a similar situation. In essence, because of our schemas we don't believe what we see, we tend to see what we already believe.

We are born with only two 'fears': a fear of loud noises, and a fear of falling. This is why you will notice a baby jump if a door slams, or a toddler instinctively putting their arms out to catch themselves if they fall. However, these fears are primarily a protection mechanism to keep us safe. They aren't linked to our 'fight, flight or freeze' mechanism unless a subsequent negative experience occurs. For example, someone who has been involved in a bomb blast might then understandably link loud noises to danger, and would react accordingly, even in a situation that wasn't dangerous. It is only when we are in a heightened state of fear, embarrassment or anxiety that our brain is provided with the evidence that we need to be protected from something, allowing a phobia, anxiety or irrational fear to develop.

This response to a frightening event is entirely down to the individual. Two people may experience the same traumatic experience, yet only one may develop a phobia, as each interprets the same event differently. Let's think of the bomb example again – one person involved may accept that this was an extreme event that is unlikely ever to happen to them again, whereas another may unconsciously choose to believe that they need to protect themselves against a similar situation in the future just in case it does occur again. In the second person, a link from loud noises to their 'fight, flight or freeze' mechanism is created, leading to phobias, anxiety, panic attacks, avoidance and fears.

Although the majority of our schemas are positive and hugely helpful in life, it is the schemas associated with incorrectly protecting us from perceived dangers that can cause us problems. If these negative schemas are not dealt with and conditioned, they can last a lifetime, with debilitating and devastating effects on the quality of your life and those around you. So you see, we are essentially the sum of all our schemas, and the bad ones can have a negative impact on how we act and feel.

Even everyday events can affect people very differently, creating different schemas within people who experience the exact same situation. For example, Eva grew up around some people who regularly abused alcohol. These people created schemas that caused them to believe that alcohol is a good way to unwind and deal with problems. Conversely, Eva's schema is: 'I can see how destructive alcohol can be, so I would never drink often or to excess.' The reason for the vast differences in people's beliefs, actions and behaviours is fundamentally a result of the fact that no matter what we observe, hear or experience, every minute of every day our minds are unconsciously asking the question, 'What does this mean to me?' The interpretation of what any event or person means to us personally is wholly based upon our existing schemas or beliefs. It is entirely individual, and therefore the resulting responses and behaviours are too.

You see, our brain interprets EVERYTHING based upon what it means to us, or how the experience could or will affect us. Our mind then makes its own interpretation and adjusts it accordingly to create our individual thought patterns and schemas. Our brain is designed to protect us at all costs and to stop us doing anything that may harm us. In a modern world, where physical dangers such as predators are now minimal, this self-protection may extend to the avoidance of feeling uncomfortable, fearful, uncertain, embarrassed or anxious.

In order to change – to be the best person, the best parent, the best spouse, the best employee, the best in your job and in your life, and to be able to achieve all those things you want to do – you may have to do things that are difficult, scary and uncertain, which can create some discomfort. This is good discomfort, and a way to move past overly protective schemas.

To be able to change your life for the better and to minimise these feelings of discomfort, you have to change your schemas, as it is they that drive your feelings and behaviours. In order to change your behaviours in a positive way, you have to positively challenge the schemas that negatively affect you.

We create so many inaccurate schemas as children, based upon beliefs that we derive from parents, friends, the media and society. Those beliefs are also often influenced by what country we are from, our race, gender, religion and social class. In essence, we could have numerous schemas that are based upon incorrect information, the opinions of others or our own incorrect interpretation of events from when we were a child.

We would like you to consider that while you cannot control events around you, what you can control is what you focus on and how you interpret things, before subsequently choosing what to do. You see, nothing has any meaning except the meaning we give it, so we need to stop being driven by old and incorrect meanings and instead to challenge all that we do. Ultimately these things control our lives. And being in control of your life is what this book is all about.

If you want to change your life, then YOU HAVE GOT TO CHANGE. After all, if nothing changes, then nothing changes!

If you want your life to get better, then you have to get better – that's the only way it happens. We therefore want to help you change old negative schemas, patterns, beliefs or behaviours in order for you to be the person you choose to be, without having to endure the internal conflict caused by wanting to behave in a certain way while being driven by incorrect schemas and influences from the past.

For instance, if you have a couple of relationships that go wrong, you could end up believing that all relationships are bad. You may choose to stay single for years and years, until you realise that, actually, it wasn't being in a relationship that was bad, it was being in a relationship with the wrong person that was bad. When that 'click' happens in your head and you stop blaming relationships and realise it is the incompatible partners that are to blame, you will feel ready to move on. You can then clearly see how wrong your old thought pattern (schema) was.

So why wait for years to turn your unhelpful thoughts around when you could do it right now? You can condition or change your old schemas with new evidence in a split second, and the new, positive, factually correct schema can then set you free.

Say, for instance, you don't trust people and you think they let you down all the time. As a result, you don't allow anyone into your life and because you're lonely you end up feeling even angrier towards people. But the more people you let in, the bigger your world becomes. We've let a lot of people into our lives over the years and, yes, some have let us down. But we learned from those people too, so our schema is that they've done us a big favour in the long run.

This process of changing what could have been perceived as a negative into a positive is something that we hope to teach you in this book. Remember, there is always an element of risk involved in every aspect of life, but risks are worth taking.

Just consider, there is also a significant risk in taking no risks. Risks create rewards, and as the saying goes, 'If you do what you've always done, then you'll get what you always got.' Risks are the opportunity for a new path and a new destiny, and after all, when you feel deep inside that your life should be better, doing nothing and expecting things to change is the biggest risk of all.

Remember, even if something does go wrong for whatever reason as you take steps to upgrade your life, it can never be classed as a failure, because, brilliantly, there's no such thing unless you quit (see Chapter Five for more on this). No matter what you do, and no matter what the outcome, you have got a result! You've just learned something from that experience. You may have just learned how not to do something, but it's still a result, as you now know what not to do, so in that sense it counts as a success.

Every bit of feedback you get means more experience, and you could say that good judgement comes from experience, and experience most often comes from bad judgement! Ultimately, the more things we do and the more risks we take, the wiser and better equipped for life we become.

If we decide to eat a strawberry and we've never eaten one before, we could discover that we're allergic to it and get ill. But, on the other hand, we could discover that it's the best thing we've ever tasted. So many people are risk averse, but remember: no risk equals no reward.

Each of us is the centre of our own universe, and it's up to us how big, small, fun, fruitful or varied that universe is. You can either make it very bland by keeping yourself locked in and being insular, or you can open your world up to so many readily available and thoroughly exciting possibilities.

The simple fact is, we're not born with any negative schemas, we create them, and anything we have created we can condition and change. We just need to know how. That's the message at the core of this book. We will share with you in the following chapters the twelve core schemas you need to enable yourself to break those debilitating habits you've been carrying around with you for years – habits you no longer want or need in your life.

A Bit About Us . . .

You may perhaps think, 'How do you know changing your schemas can upgrade your life? What's your proof?' So we would like to tell you a bit about ourselves so you fully understand where we're coming from.

We met in 1991, and like any relationship, ours hasn't always been perfect, but in hard times we've always taken a step back and evaluated how it can be better. In doing so, we've questioned everything and adapted our beliefs to make things work. As a result of that, we've created the twelve core schemas that you're going to learn about (and then we sincerely hope you will use!) in this book.

In order for you to fully understand how we got to where we are today, we feel that it's important to tell you a bit about our background, both as individuals and as a couple. People often look at us now and say things like, 'You're so lucky,' but there is no such thing as random luck. We create our life, and we create our own luck! There is a great saying, 'The harder you work, the luckier you get', and this really is true. So by sharing our life story with you, we hope you will see that we, like most, have had our own obstacles to overcome, but we've managed to turn things around and have totally transformed our lives as a result. We've dissected all the negative beliefs we held and turned them into positives, and this book is all about showing how you can do the same.

Eva's story

I was born into a Polish family. We didn't speak English at home and when I started school, aged four, I immediately felt very different. I was shy and, maybe because of the language barrier, I fell behind academically. I felt isolated from my classmates and like I didn't fit in.

I had kidney failure when I was seven and as a result ended up in hospital for many weeks. There was a very real possibility that I could die and I recall that at this time I got lots of attention. I remember getting a Girl's World (a doll's head to apply make-up on, which I had always wanted) and it wasn't even Christmas or my birthday!

My older sister loved me and must have been worried that she might lose her little sister, but she was also only a child who couldn't help feeling neglected by our parents as a result of all the attention I was getting and their frequent hospital visits to see me. I felt this caused issues in our relationship.

When I reached my early teens I was really grateful that my parents recognised that I was struggling academically, and they arranged for me to have a private tutor so I could keep up with the other pupils. It was then that I flourished at school. However, because I started to do really well in my classes, I then got bullied because the kids thought I was a swot.

I was also a little plump as a teenager, so I got called 'fat' and 'pregnant' and that affected me very badly. I had been brought up a Catholic, and as such had very strong views with regards to underage sex and promiscuity. This hurtful and untrue pregnancy gossip spread through the school like wildfire. I loved my teachers and their encouragement and praise for the standard of my work, but I was terrified of the gossip and didn't want to go to school. Despite quietly enduring years of bullying at high school, which I never said a word about to my mum, I decided to speak to her on this occasion. Like me, my mum was furious, and for the first and only time she went to school to see my head teacher over a negative issue and to insist it was resolved, which it was.

After school I went to college and met my first boyfriend, who was very sweet. However, that fell apart when he cheated on me, and I felt totally crushed. My self-esteem and confidence spiralled even lower, and this gave the schema I'd created at school that I was fat and ugly even more gravitas. This infidelity provided me with evidence that all the derogatory things I believed about myself must be true.

Believing that how I looked must have caused him to cheat, I went on to become obsessed with losing weight. My weight plummeted and, as is often the case with anorexia, my clothes became baggier to hide my skeletal frame. I then met my second boyfriend. He was a big drinker and also very violent, but because I'd seen that behaviour before, I assumed it was acceptable. I made excuses for the way he acted and rationalised it. I blamed the drink and his friends, justifying how awful he was by telling myself that he loved me, while ignoring huge evidence to the contrary.

Our understanding of behaviour is based upon what we see, in the same way that you know an apple is an apple because you've been told and shown that it is. My definition of love had been shaped by my personal experience. I had witnessed someone close to me being physically assaulted, and then told they were loved seconds later. That then became my learning (schema) for love, and why I believed that violence in a relationship must be acceptable.

After numerous acts of violence against me, things got so bad that my boyfriend headbutted me and fractured my skull. I've never felt such excruciating pain in my life. I was in a nightclub, and I was so ashamed. I blamed myself and felt people would judge me, thinking I must have provoked his attack. I was so glad my cousin was there. She took me straight to hospital, and I just have a hazy memory of pain and begging them to please take it away. I was in such agony and felt such despair that I didn't know how I could come back from it. I had got myself into such a destructive situation and I was so incredibly unhappy.

My self-esteem was on the floor and I knew I was losing the fight to want to carry on living. I didn't have the emotional skills to get through it. Or at least I didn't think so. But what I've learned in life is that you always have options, no matter how bad or dark things may seem. Looking back, although what happened was very traumatic, once I recovered even the smallest amount of strength, I knew I had to turn things around or I'd forever be in a similar situation.

That event and all the other negative things that were happening in my life at the time helped to teach me what I didn't want in life. They also made me start thinking about what I did want and how I could make my life better. I felt empowered by the fact that I had made a decision to take action, and I accepted responsibility for everything that had happened to me. I couldn't change any of those events, but what I could change was my perception of those events.

I started to learn that, no matter what happens in life, there would be only one person with me twenty-four hours a day, seven days a week, for the rest of my life, and that person was ME. As soon as I had this realisation, I started to move on and change the patterns that were marring my life.

Nik's story

I have a similar story to Eva in that I was a very ill child. I had terrible eczema, and from an early age I was seeing doctor after doctor, none of whom offered my parents much help, other than various steroid creams. The greatest reassurance my parents were offered was that perhaps I would 'grow out of it'. I used to go to bed with several different creams and ointments on my skin, and I'd be wrapped up in bandages like a mummy to stop me scratching at my body.

My parents devoted themselves to me and my brother, who is two years older than me. Until I was born, everything had been about him. He was the centre of my parents' universe before I came along. Apparently, a few weeks after bringing me home from hospital, my brother asked my parents to please take me back. However, as he was just two, that was entirely understandable, because when I arrived I began getting some of the attention that had been all his and, being a baby, I wasn't even fun to play with.

Looking back, I feel very sorry for my brother, as not only did I disrupt his world and take most of the attention he'd had from my parents, but when I was about five I compounded the situation by developing severe asthma. One of my earliest memories is of a family holiday to Blackpool. On the day we arrived I had such a bad asthma attack that I had to spend the entire time in hospital, initially in intensive care. Of course, my brother was too young to understand that I was ill, and as far as he was concerned I'd totally ruined his holiday. He didn't get to enjoy all the fun of the Pleasure Beach because my parents spent most of the time by my bedside. It must have been so difficult for him.

Throughout my schooldays I was constantly on steroid tablets or injections and antibiotics due to my asthma. My mum had seen me nearly die twice so understandably she became overprotective of me and always used to say that she had to 'wrap me up in cotton wool to keep me safe'. The slightest sniffle meant that she kept me home from school, resulting in my school attendance being very low.

I didn't have many friends at school because I was ill so often that I didn't have the time to develop friendships. As a result my childhood felt very restricted compared to that of others.

The first turning point in my life came in 1977 when I was sixteen and I was watching *The Russell Harty Show*. Arnold Schwarzenegger was a guest on the show, promoting a film called *Pumping Iron*. From the moment I saw him he amazed me. How could someone become so fit and muscular? I was this frail little boy who was immensely thin and was being bullied at school. On top of that a chest infection could be fatal, so Mum didn't really want me playing outside in cold weather. That one interview made me stop and think, 'Do I really have to put up with this? Is this how my life is going to be forever, or can I do something about it?'

In that moment I started to reconsider my way of thinking. I started reading about Arnold Schwarzenegger and he inspired me to change. We'll talk about his story in more detail later in the book (see page 138), but to this day he remains my biggest role model.

Off the back of my newfound love and respect for Arnie, when I was able I decided to start bodybuilding. My dad was also very much into keeping fit (or 'physical culture' as he used to call it), as he had previously been inspired by Charles Atlas. I began using his chest expanders and other gym equipment, and dreamed of being fit and healthy for the first time in my life, as I now believed that good health could quite possibly be a choice.

I wasn't particularly knowledgeable about bodybuilding, but I knew that to build more muscle in my body I needed to eat more protein. It was not possible to consume the amount of protein required just from food, and therefore I looked at supplementing my intake with protein powders, which back then in the seventies were high in dairy derivatives; furthermore, it was common practice to mix them with milk. Sadly, I wasn't aware of the damage that all the years of antibiotics and steroids had done to my body and particularly my bowel. Also, unbeknown to me at the time, drinking milk was the worst thing I could have done.

Having overcome my eczema and reached a point where I was successfully managing my asthma, by the age of twenty I became very ill again. I started to lose blood when I went to the toilet, which, being a typical guy, I initially ignored, hoping it would get better by itself, until one day I collapsed and was admitted to hospital. I felt so ill I honestly thought I was dying. I had ignored the fact that my abdomen was swollen, my skin had gradually turned grey and I had become incredibly lethargic. I didn't even feel I had the energy to fight whatever was happening to me. In hospital I had a barium enema, and they diagnosed me with a chronic inflammatory bowel disease, ulcerative colitis, which affects the lining of the large intestine and rectum. Ulcers and abscesses develop, and these cause bloody stools, diarrhoea and abdominal pain.

My body had become toxic, hence the reason my skin had gone grey, as I was being poisoned by my waste via the open abscesses and ulcers. The consultant gastroenterologist said it was so bad that toxic megacolon had begun to set in, and therefore they would have to remove my bowel otherwise the poisoning would kill me, or my colon would rupture within weeks.

A specialist came to my bedside and talked me through the proctocolectomy and ileostomy, followed by living with a colostomy bag. I was naturally horrified at the thought of having to have such a huge operation at such a young age, one that would change my life forever. I had the benefit of private medical insurance, but despite being under one of the top consultants in the country, I was told that there was no other option available to me as all the medication, steroids, steroid enemas and anti-inflammatories were just not working.

I was at the lowest point of my life, and I remember lying in hospital thinking I'd had enough. I felt there had to be another way to get better, other than having such a major operation and a colostomy bag. People were discovering and learning new things every day and I believed that someone, somewhere would have an answer.

My dad frequently told me, 'There is always a way, and the answers to anything you need to know are in the library,' so I made a decision to find a way to get better. I signed myself out of hospital, and I went to the library and read up on everything I possibly could about the digestive system. I came to the conclusion that there is a lot of truth in the saying, 'You are what you eat.' I wasn't born with my bowel problem; it developed because my bowel had been inadvertently abused as a side effect of all the prescription medication I had taken as a child.

I decided to completely fast for one week and have nothing but water to see what impact that would have, as I figured open ulcers and abscesses would not heal if waste was constantly passing over them. Gradually I started to feel a little better. I read that one of the least intrusive foods you can ingest is long-grain brown rice, and it is also a great complex carbohydrate, so I lived off a small amount four to six times a day.

My health began to recover, and as it did I then added other foods into my diet one at a time to see if I could tolerate them. This helped me to categorise foods into those that healed me, those that gave me energy and those that made me ill. The day I tried milk again I was cripplingly ill within an hour. The excruciating pain resurfaced, and that was when I discovered that milk and dairy products had quite literally been killing me.

After a year, as I got better, I was able to reduce my anti-inflammatory medication until I eventually stopped it altogether. While I was thrilled with my new discovery, I was also angry at the hospital consultant for only offering me what would have been a life-altering surgery as a solution to save my life. I do appreciate now that this was offered with the absolute best of intentions, and my approach may not have worked for others. However, I went back to see him to share my medical transformation and ask him why he pursued such drastic action, which at that time I perceived could potentially ruin my life. He had no real answers, and just kept saying that he wanted to 'save my life'. This changed my perspective as my anger was transformed into a massive realisation that he was right. He only knew what he had been taught, and he had been taught that the only way my life could be saved was to remove my bowel! Furthermore, he was a surgeon and his job, in the simplest of terms, was to cut people open and remove or fix what was going wrong; it was not to look for or really consider alternatives.

Of course I'm not saying for a minute here that you shouldn't listen to what doctors say, because they are the experts and they're trying to help you, but if you are not happy with what you are told then please do get a second opinion or discuss alternatives with another health practitioner. Medical science is constantly developing, with new treatments, interpretations and strategies emerging all the time. If you believe there is another way, then you are within your rights to explore it, and look for other options and alternatives.

From that day forward I changed my belief system 100 per cent and decided to start listening to myself more. I researched everything I could, looking for different ideas, answers and viewpoints, and basically stopped letting other people dictate my life. For so many people, life is what happens to them; it is not what they make happen. They're told what to do and think according to the rules, views and standards imposed by their employer, the TV, their parents or their partner.

My dad was a massive role model to me growing up because he had a schema that there was nothing that couldn't be fixed. I had now experienced this myself with my chronic ulcerative colitis. He always worked hard and focused on what he wanted, and if things went wrong, he made them right, so he was an amazing person to learn from. He didn't moan and he didn't feel sorry for himself whatever happened to him; he just found a way to make things work.

During that period of time after my illness I changed from being someone who was sick and dying to someone who knew and believed that anything was possible, and I have been that way ever since.

Nik and Eva: the day we met

The day we met changed both of our lives forever, and for the better. Here's the story of how we found each other and what happened next.

EVA

When Nik and I met I was working in a bank, and because he was a financial advisor, I would visit his office to try to encourage him to use our banking facilities for his clients.

When I first met him I thought he was overconfident and perhaps even a bit arrogant. But all that changed one day when my car got stolen from outside his office. I was only twenty-one, in a new job with a beautiful company car, and Nik was a complete knight in shining armour to me.

He was due to go to America in the early hours of the following morning, yet instead of going home and packing, he was busy looking after me and making sure that everything got sorted out. I was so grateful that I offered to take him out for lunch to say thank you once he returned from America. It was all meant completely innocently, but we instantly hit it off.

In view of what had happened to Nik years earlier with his health, he questioned behaviours and habits, which led him to study psychology, nutrition and self-development. He talked about it so passionately that it kick-started something in me too.

Nik told me how, at the age of twenty-two, he had formed a goal to read a new psychology or self-development book every week, which he had continued to do. In fact, the first time we went on holiday together as a couple he gave me a self-development tape to listen to while I was sunbathing by the pool. I was a bit cynical, but it turned out to be fascinating. The guy on the tape talked about how important it is to **plan your life**, something that I'd never considered before. When I finished listening, Nik asked me if I would be willing to plan my life with him if we stayed together.

From that day onwards we started writing down all of our goals. It was such a turning point for me, and also for us as a couple. Before then no one had ever asked me what I wanted in life. I knew what I didn't want, but I'd never considered what my future plans were. I had a good job and I was doing well for myself, but I was kind of plodding along, hoping for the best. It never crossed my mind that I could decide everything that my future would hold.

I maintained a healthy scepticism, but two weeks later something incredible happened: one of the things I'd written down on my list came true. Then suddenly other things started to come true too. It was like magic, and I was hooked! I now had the knowledge that I could create my own path, and I realised that if I didn't plan my life, I would be working to someone else's plan. That knowledge was the first step to fulfilment, and it is still incredibly powerful.

NIK

When Eva and I met we realised that we both wanted our lives to have more depth and meaning than either of us had ever experienced before. We had both had relationships that didn't work, and we didn't want to repeat those patterns.

Prior to meeting Eva, I had been in a relationship for some years, and while some relationships grow together over the years, some unfortunately grow apart. We were both young when we met and sadly our relationship did the latter.

When Eva and I met, we decided that if we were going to enter into a relationship, we were going to do it right and set ourselves up for the rest of our lives. While we could both have easily slipped into just another relationship and carried on that pattern forever, we documented the lessons we had both learned and agreed that we were ready to change.

People sometimes say to us, 'Well, it's all right for you because your relationship is great,' but that's because we found ways to create it like that. We both decided that communication is the main component and absolutely paramount to a healthy relationship. We made shared decisions and both gave equal commitment to them. Together we learned that we are all masters of our own destiny, but we often give others power over us.

Until she met me, Eva thought everything was in the lap of the gods, and she was floating along waiting for things to happen. But she discovered that she could decide what the rest of her life held for her, and she acted upon that and everything changed for the better.

We're still 'normal', though, and over the years we've endured ups and downs, because life is what it is and no one is immune to good or bad things happening to them. We will always be affected by external events, whether personal, such as the loss of a loved one, or global, such as the COVID-19 pandemic, but it's how you choose to view them and subsequently how you deal with them that counts.

Since we developed our system, our dreams have been unlocked and come true. We have an amazing home and two incredible children, we're both healthy and we are constantly working to get our message across that there is always a way and there is always hope. We want to get this message to as many people as possible via as many mediums as we can. We're changing lives daily, and with scientific studies into our therapy we hope that in the not-too-distant future it can be shared with other psychologists and therapists, allowing more and more people to benefit and overcome their issues. We help people in our private practice, on TV, online via our YouTube videos and with various social media channels. We write books, have our podcast *Making the Change* and we host workshops around the world so we can reach out and help more and more people. It's everything we planned for, all that we created, and it certainly hasn't happened by chance.

The Tools:
Our Twelve
Core Schemas

The twelve core schemas, which are the basis of the chapters that follow in this book, came to us during a series of conversations early on in our relationship. Eva was still reeling from her bad relationship, she was angry towards certain family members and the school bully, and she also felt resentful about challenges she felt she had faced at home. She was most of all angry with herself for having put up with so much, and felt so much shame and regret for things that had happened in the past.

Likewise, Nik was still recovering from the breakdown of his relationship, and he was still working hard at trying not to feel like a victim due to his prior illnesses.

When we considered it, we realised that all of these thoughts and feelings about the past, and about those we felt had done us wrong, were literally doing us no favours at all. The negative events had happened and we couldn't do anything to change them now, but the blame and regret were two emotions that we continued to inflict upon ourselves long after the events were over. Until we learned a new way to move on.

Through the process of getting to know each other we learned so much, and we then sat down and wrote a plan for our life together. It's as simple as that. You plan short-term things like going on holiday the following year, but we also decided to plan everything in the long term too.

We looked at everything, from where we wanted to live to even how long we wanted to live. We looked at things that may hold us back in an emotional sense and worked out where we had put up invisible barriers due to negative events in our past that had created schemas, and the best ways to break them down. Since then, nothing has stopped us.

We were aware that there would be a transitional period to start with and that old behavioural patterns would try to keep us in the past. This is always the case if you've had the same schemas for a long time, as behaviour and thought processes also become habitual. But we learned as we went along and lived by the rule that if someone in the world had done something that we wanted to do, then anyone, including us, could do it too. Every time we came across an obstacle or something that wasn't working as we wanted it to, we questioned why and then readjusted our thinking and approach.

The most important realisation we had was that the first thing we needed to do was take responsibility for everything that had happened in our lives and to stop blaming other people. We also had to ask why we didn't believe we could do certain things, and what was holding us back. Once we had those two core schemas in place, the other ten followed naturally.

Quite honestly, developing our core schemas did take a lot of work, and then accepting, believing and practising them took even more, as getting to grips with them doesn't happen overnight for everyone. In fact, at first, we found it hard to believe schema 9 (save yourself before you save the world) and schema 10 (no one is born bad), even though we knew that believing them would add greater depth to our lives. But if you are willing to practise and use them as life-changing affirmations, as you will find at the end of each chapter, they can work for you too. The outcome is so worth it because you're setting yourself up for the rest of your life.

We are not ruling out the possibility that in the future we may have more schemas to add, but the twelve listed below are a foundation to build upon, and they're the basic ones we believe everyone needs to know.

You may even come up with some new schemas of your own while reading this book, and that's how it should be, because it shows that you're taking control of your life and understanding what's holding you back all on your own.

The twelve core schemas

1. **There is no one reality.**

2. **Disregard the doubters.**

3. **Accept responsibility.**

4. **Anything is possible.**

5. **Failure only exists when you quit.**

6. **It's never too late.**

7. **Plan your life.**

8. **You are what you eat.**

9. **Save yourself before you save the world.**

10. **No one is born bad.**

11. **You've got to give to receive.**

12. **You become what you think about.**

We're sure that you may already agree with, or at least identify with, some of the schemas above. You may also already disagree with one or two, as we did initially too. However, over the next twelve chapters we are going to explain exactly what they mean, how they can benefit you and how you can start integrating them into your everyday life in a very easy way.

We're going to give you compelling evidence that should make your acceptance of these core schemas quite simple, but you will – as we did – have to practise them often. This book is quite simply about YOU helping yourself and transforming your life from what it is right now to what you have always wanted it to be.

1

There Is No One Reality

The first of our schemas is this: **there is no one reality**. Some people find this statement challenging, but we believe it's essential to look at every situation from more than one point of view.

When we encounter a situation, whether it is a new experience or one we have had many times before, we instinctively apply our view of the world, our life skills and our knowledge to that situation and immediately make an assumption based on our personal experiences. Our brain is doing its best with the information it has, but it can get things very wrong. For example, you might have personally experienced the situation of not having heard from a friend for a while and are wondering if you've upset them in any way, questioning your last interaction. Then suddenly out of the blue your friend calls to say that their mobile broke and they've been waiting for a replacement, so you've spent that time worrying and getting anxious unnecessarily.

Think about it. If life was simple, and there was only ever one reality, we wouldn't need a judicial system. That's why we have a jury, so they can be impartial when both sides feel they're both absolutely right in what they believe. People are prepared to spend thousands, sometimes millions, on lawyers' fees because they are so convinced that they are right. The amazing thing is that the opposing side thinks the same too!

We once worked with a doctor from Scotland who was involved in a study examining the effect of placebos on pain control. Ten patients, all of whom were in severe pain, were being treated with morphine. They were asked if they would like to participate in a study of a ground-breaking new type of morphine. All of them signed up.

Every day a doctor visited them and injected them with this new wonder morphine. It was actually normal morphine but a slightly higher dose, and as expected all participants reported that they were pain-free. However, on day four, unbeknown to the participants, they were injected with a placebo that was quite simply a coloured saline solution that looked like the previous morphine. That continued for an entire month, and by the end of the month nine of the ten participants remained pain-free. The tenth person, while considerably better, was still experiencing moderate pain. This experiment was a testament to the absolute power of belief. Because the participants believed they were being injected with a new pain-killing wonder drug, the majority remained pain-free.

The patients' pain was a reality. But so was their belief in a cure.

If a person has a crippling fear of spiders and they go to their doctor, they may be given anti-anxiety drugs that make them feel less anxious. However, if you take away that medication, the fear is still there. They are still scared. This is because the medication merely reduces the anxiety, which is the symptomatic behaviour. It does not eradicate the cause and therefore the medication is simply masking the problem.

A lady once said to Eva, 'You're so lucky, you're naturally slim.' Eva had never realised people thought that about her because the reality is that she was an overweight teenager and it was only around the time she met Nik that she became slim, as she started to exercise and take an interest in eating well to become healthier. These days she goes to the gym four or five times a week and eats healthily, and she's open about the fact that she works hard to stay in shape. Her reality is that she works very hard to stay slim, but the other lady's reality is that it's completely effortless and Eva was born that way.

Understanding that **there is no one reality** is also a way putting things into perspective. We had a leak in our roof recently, and instead of thinking, 'Oh my God! We could have done without that,' we thought, 'We are very fortunate to have a big roof, so we were sure to get a leak one day. No problem, we can get it fixed.' Knowing that we can choose a different reality means we can spin situations around and restructure them with a positive slant. It's not always easy to do when you're feeling angry about something, but once you feel calmer and you can take a step back, you can consider looking at things from a different perspective by creating a 'new' reality.

Shakespeare wrote in *Hamlet*, 'There is nothing either good or bad, but thinking makes it so.' He is absolutely correct and the great thing about your thoughts is that you are 100 per cent in control of them. You and you alone choose how you wish to interpret any events in your life. So, if you don't like a situation, either move away from it or look at it differently until you find a way that feels better.

Thoughts become feelings, and feelings dictate actions; actions dictate behaviours and persistent behaviours create habits. Every single time people come to see us about a bad relationship they're getting over, we ask them if they would rather have never gone through it. Nine times out of ten they say they would rather have gone through it and learned the lessons they did than to have skipped it altogether – no matter how bad it was. But, of course, when you're in that bad relationship you can't see anything positive coming out of it.

*

Schemas mean we don't believe what we see, we see what we already believe. Whether it's right or wrong, it's our individual belief and we have a habit of clinging to it!

In 2015 a photograph became a viral phenomenon all over the world. Cecilia Bleasdale took a photograph of a dress she had seen and planned to wear to her daughter's wedding. She sent the picture to her daughter for her thoughts, yet mum and daughter had a disagreement as to the colour of the dress.

Due to the conflict over the actual colour of the dress, the bride decided to prove a point with her mum and post a photograph of the dress on her Facebook page to gather the support of her friends. Incredibly, her friends also disagreed over the colour. Some saw the dress as white with gold lace, while others saw it as blue with black lace.

We now discuss this case at our workshops and while the bulk of the room see white and gold, many see blue and black. If you are not familiar with the dress then just search 'white gold, blue black dress' and see what you see. Eva actually sees the dress as white and gold, yet Nik sees the very same dress as blue and black. The truth is, it's the same dress, yet we have entirely different experiences of its colour in the image and we are both right, thus proving that, quite literally, **there is no one reality**!

Over the years we have been fortunate enough to have worked with numerous lottery winners, many of whom have experienced very mixed emotions. On the one hand, they're deliriously happy they've got money, security and perceived happiness, but the flip side is that it becomes incredibly hard to know who to trust and, even more so, how to deal with the expectations of friends or family, particularly if they're struggling financially.

If someone wins £5 million, for example, and they generously give their close relatives £50,000 each, while some recipients may be thrilled, others may think they're stingy and will speak badly about them to friends and family. It's £50,000! That kind of thing can transform lives for the better, or in other realities it can cause family in-fighting, leaving the lottery winners feeling sadder and more confused than before they won the money.

It just shows how differently people can react to an identical situation. No matter how hard you try to do the right thing, it will mean the world to some and never be enough for others, and that simply comes down to the way they perceive things.

Just imagine that for many years you have visited the same local pub and then you win £1 million on the lottery, so the next time you go in, you kindly want to buy drinks for everyone. Now, while some people would think you're amazingly generous, others would think you're a self-important big shot. It is impossible to please everyone. You therefore have to live your life the way you think is best for you and try not to think too hard about the consequences. People will always perceive things differently to you, and you can't keep everyone smiling all of the time. It's just the way the world works.

Your Attitude Is Your Choice

Today is the day you need to get a happier, more positive attitude. Why? Well, give us one good reason why not? We know you deserve it!

It's so easy to get caught up in the loop of spending so much time focusing on things that go wrong in our lives. For example, we may have ten tasks in a day, but if one of those tasks goes wrong, we often waste so much time dwelling on and feeling bad about it, instead of focusing on the nine tasks that went right.

We've spoken to so many celebrities who say that when they go on social media they can read a hundred or more lovely messages from people, but as soon as they read a negative one, it can ruin their entire day. When they go to bed that night, it's the negative message that they're thinking about, not all the great things that have happened to them that day or the hundreds of messages that were lovely. If you think about it, it doesn't really make any sense. We are essentially striving for everyone to like us, but please take note: you will NEVER get everyone to like you – that's simply impossible. So right now, make a decision to let this thought go, free yourself from the burden of trying to please everyone, accept that you can always just do your best and if someone doesn't like it, then that is 100 per cent their problem and, furthermore, what they think is none of your business.

We are socially conditioned to concentrate on what goes wrong as opposed to what goes right, and this all begins when we start at school. Just consider how we used to get little ticks when we did something right, yet huge angry crosses, often in red, when we did something wrong, focusing our attention on that. While this way of thinking starts at a very young age, it's never too late to change it.

A lady we had worked with called Jo had been friends with Sam for over twenty years. Jo had always suffered from low self-esteem, and all the time they had been friends Jo had remembered a comment that Sam had made about 'none of their friendship group being anything special looks-wise'. As a teenager Jo had taken this to mean that Sam didn't think she was very attractive, and she'd let it eat away at her a little every time she thought about it.

Many years later, Jo decided to bring it up over a couple of glasses of wine and laughed as she remembered the time Sam effectively said their group of friends were frankly rather plain. Sam was absolutely horrified. She couldn't even remember making the comment and admitted that she'd always felt like the ugly one in the group because everyone else was so pretty. Jo had been carrying that throwaway comment around for all those years, when the reality was that Sam was the one who didn't feel good enough. Even though it was such a small thing, this new factual information provided an entirely new reality for Jo. As such, this alternative reality gave her self-esteem a huge boost that day, because she was able to let go of the past and move forward.

Another example is the story of a client whose mum had died when she was a little girl. From that moment on, her world had become a nightmare. She admitted that it was chaos in her house when she was young and everyone was trying to get to bed. There were five children, and it used to be her mum who would look after everyone and ensure the bedtime procedure ran smoothly. After her mum passed away, every night at 9 p.m. her dad would turn off all the electricity in the house and send all the kids to bed without so much as a kiss or a 'goodnight'. She had so much anger and resentment towards him because she felt like he didn't care about her or her siblings. She perceived his method as callous and loveless and couldn't see it any other way until we asked her, 'Could it be that your dad worked all day, came in tired, fed you all, and when he asked you to go to bed, you all ran riot? Maybe the only way he could deal with getting you all to bed at once was by pulling the power so you had no choice.' We pointed out, 'That may have been the hardest time of day for him as well, because he probably missed your mum at night more than ever.'

The years of hatred and resentment melted away in front of our eyes. She admitted that she found it hard enough to deal with her own two children at bedtime, let alone all of the screaming kids he had had to put up with. Her reality suddenly changed from resentment to compassion towards her father. She started to see things from his point of view and realised that he didn't turn off the electricity to be cruel. He just found everything too much to deal with.

Something similar happened with another of our clients, a lady called Amanda. She had a very high-powered job, but she was drinking so much that she was effectively an alcoholic. It had got to the point where she was drinking wine every day to suppress her anger and sadness. She saw getting drunk as the only way to deal with her emotions.

Amanda said the drinking had started slowly, with a bottle of wine a day, and had developed into three bottles on some days. The problem began when her dad died and she offered to build an annexe onto the side of her house for her mum to live in. She told us that she absolutely hated her mother but felt obliged to take care of her as she was an only child. Seeing her mum or hearing her voice infuriated Amanda so much that the only way she could deal with it was by getting drunk every night. She went on to explain how her dad had been a violent drinker when she was growing up, and whenever he got into one of his rages, no matter what time of night it was, her mum would go up to Amanda's room, close the door and drag her heavy chest of drawers in front of it, and then her dad would bang on the door and shout behind it. Her actual words about her mother were: 'She continually brought trouble to my door.' She believed her mum was a bitch for always bringing 'a madman' to the door of her bedroom.

After listening to Amanda's story, we asked her a question: 'What would you do if a madman ever broke into your house?' She replied, 'I would protect my children.' We went on to ask, 'So if your children were in bed, what would you do?' Amanda responded, 'Run upstairs to their bedroom and lock the door!' We then went silent and waited for her to realise what she had said and how that related to her and her mum. It took a couple of minutes for her to process this new information, but when she did it was amazing. She realised her mum hadn't locked herself in her daughter's room with the intention of enticing her drunk, violent dad upstairs to her door. She had done it simply to protect her.

As soon as Amanda could see this new, more positive perspective, her anger entirely dissipated and she felt calm. As a result, her relationship with her mum improved tenfold. She also reduced her drinking, eventually stopping altogether as she no longer needed to self-medicate with alcohol. Her perceived reality was that her mum didn't care for her, but in fact she cared about her so much that her first instinct was always to protect her.

Terminology

Thinking the worst or being negative is a learned behaviour, and that becomes habitual. It's time to break that habit – perhaps it's long overdue!

To start changing this immediately, the moment you have a negative thought or opinion, quickly add '*but luckily . . .*' and then conclude the sentence. These two words will force you to seek a positive conclusion to that sentence or thought. By using it consistently it will help you to create new neural pathways in your brain, so it becomes second nature.

Using 'but luckily . . .' to conclude any negative thought or statement forces you to find a more positive outcome. They're just two words that can transform your negative thoughts, words and habits.

For example:

'That's not the way I would do it, *but luckily* I can show them my way, as perhaps they haven't considered that.'

'It's raining again, *but luckily* I have an umbrella.'

'Today has been a total disaster, *but luckily* tomorrow I can start to put those situations right.'

Another example that will help you adopt a more positive reality with regards to people who have wronged or upset you is considering:

'It's not their fault, they're just products of their environment.'

Practice makes perfect. You can create new habits by adopting new behaviours. Initially this will take conscious effort, but eventually it will become an unconscious habit.

Exercise

Consider negative statements that you frequently use and note them down in the table opposite. It's a good idea to place a marker or bookmark on that page so you can add to this table over the next few days and weeks, when you find yourself using negative terminology.

The terminology we use is habitual, and therefore to create new habits we first have to become consciously aware of the words we use, and then consciously employ more positive words and statements to express ourselves. The table should help you to do this.

Negative statements I frequently use	What could I say that is more positive?
Examples: I can't do this; I hate . . . ; I won't . . . ; I'll never . . .	Examples: I will learn how to do this; but luckily . . . ; I can . . . ; I will . . . ; fortunately . . .

Affirmations

> *'Nothing is good or bad, it's only my thoughts that make it so.'*

> *'I am in complete control of my thoughts and if, through previous habits, I think a negative thought, I can immediately change that by adding the words, "but luckily . . .".'*

> *'My new positive thoughts will create a new positive life for me.'*

2

Disregard
the Doubters

Our second core schema is to **disregard the doubters**. Easier said than done, you think? Well, read on, because we'll show you how it can be done.

Some years ago we were having dinner with our close friends of many years, Matthew and Jean. During dinner we were talking with real excitement about our therapy and the amazing results we were achieving. The conversation led to our thoughts for the future, and we shared how we felt that people were suffering unnecessarily. We told our friends that we wanted to bring hope to others by demonstrating our therapy's effectiveness on television and in the media, in order for people to realise that there is always hope and to therefore change more people's lives. Our friend Matthew's demeanour immediately altered, and in a very benevolent and parental manner he said, 'Listen, we care about you, and we believe in you, but you've got to be realistic and face facts: everyone would like to get into the media and TV, but it's just not easy, and to be honest, it's highly unlikely.'

Matthew then went on to say that, as a lawyer, he had represented a number of actors, and as a result he knew at first-hand the difficulty of getting jobs in television and the media. Although his comments didn't feel great to hear, what he said actually made sense to us in terms of why he had such a negative opinion about our chances. He was utilising his personal references (or schemas) from his actor clients to advise us.

We could have assumed that Matthew had a better grasp of the media world than ourselves (at the time we did not know anyone in TV or the media at all), accepted his advice and given up. But while we knew that the comments were made with the best of intentions, we reminded ourselves that we weren't actors, and we had as good a chance as anyone of getting on television to share our therapy and approach.

Had we listened to Matthew's words of caution, we would not have helped the many hundreds of people that we have worked with through the medium of television or the tens of thousands of clients we have seen privately over the years and at our workshops, as none of them would have known that we or our therapies even existed. Furthermore, our therapies would not now be in the process of being scientifically studied by universities in the Netherlands with a view to sharing them with the world.

Today, Matthew and Jean are still two of our dearest and best friends, and they're so incredibly proud of us. They often refer to that day, and also tell others about the day they told us to give up our mission to work in the media, and how we had proved them wrong. They are now two of our greatest supporters, and they always say that no matter what we do, no matter how crazy or improbable it sounds, they know that we will achieve it.

It's so important to **disregard the doubters**, as people can only give you an opinion based on their own life experiences, knowledge and skills, and even whether or not it is something they would personally consider. This often means that they simply do not have the expertise to comment on your personal situation, desires and goals.

Motives for Doubt

Remember that those casting doubt on your dreams and ambitions may not do so for the reasons you think. The motive behind anyone offering doubt can fall into one or more of the following five categories:

I wouldn't be able to do that

This is an opinion based upon a person's own learning, experiences, intellect and ability. Naturally, an opinion can only be given based upon these references. For example, if your singing abilities are not too great and you were asked to sing karaoke, you most probably would not do it.

Your own fear of singing may lead you to tell someone else that singing karaoke is a really bad idea as they can set themselves up for ridicule, when in actual fact they have an amazing voice and would really be setting themselves up for praise!

I might lose you

Sometimes doubt can be expressed out of fear of loss. For example, you may dissuade your husband, wife or partner to apply for a promotion at work due to feeling insecure and worried that a new job could result in them spending less time with you and perhaps meeting new people. If you are very insecure, you may even be fearful that they may find someone else to have a relationship with.

From what I know

Some people just like to appear as though they know everything. It gives them purpose and significance, so they comment on your choices to fulfil their needs as opposed to yours.

For example, if you wanted to be an actor, instead of agreeing with you about the great lives actors may have, they will quote just one person who regrets going into acting and then go on to tell you all the ways in which acting ruined that person's life.

I couldn't cope seeing someone else living the dreams I want

Sadly, some people will cast a shadow on your dreams just because they find it hard to cope seeing other people living their dreams. Many people don't have the drive to take action, or they have low self-esteem or low confidence and so do not feel able to do anywhere near as much as others. This is hard for them as they become envious, and to protect themselves they may try to sabotage your plans to help them feel better about themselves. Of course, this is not personal, and is often an instinctive self-protective response as opposed to one born out of malice.

I hate anyone doing well

Some people just don't like to see others doing well. Avoid these people at all costs! You should always **disregard the doubters** and follow your dreams. If someone else can't see or respect your dreams, it's entirely because they are not their dreams, so you don't need their approval or validation. As we have said before, only you will be with you every moment of every day for the rest of your life, therefore other people's opinions should never dissuade you from fulfilling your goals.

Thankfully, They Disregarded the Doubters

You really would be surprised at some of the incredible people who could so easily have quit had they listened to the doubters!

DAME JUDI DENCH

Having won an Oscar and six BAFTAs and starred in more than fifty big-screen roles, Dame Judi Dench is one of the UK's most incredible and accomplished actors, yet at the start of her career one director told Judi, 'I'm sorry, you won't ever make a film because your face is wrongly arranged.' Had Judi listened, we would never have known her or had the pleasure of enjoying her remarkable performances.

OPRAH WINFREY

Oprah Winfrey was fired from her job as a news anchor in the early 1980s for getting 'too emotionally invested' in the stories. Unbelievably, her boss at the time dismissed her as he said that she was 'unfit for TV news'. Oprah proved her boss wrong on an epic scale, as she went on to host a daytime show for twenty-five years, before launching her own TV channel. Oprah is now considered to be one of the most influential women in the world and is believed to be worth over $3 billion.

HARRISON FORD

At the age of twenty-four, Harrison Ford was told by a studio boss, 'You're never going to make it in the business. Just forget about it.' Yet he is still acting after a long and successful career that has seen him star in numerous blockbusters, such as *Star Wars*, *Patriot Games* and *Indiana Jones*. He revived his role as Han Solo in the 2015 film *Star*

Wars: The Force Awakens. Even at the age of seventy-five, he played Rick Deckard in *Blade Runner 2049*, reviving his character from the 1982 cult film *Blade Runner*. With him recently filming his fifth *Indiana Jones* instalment for release in 2023, this movie icon has well and truly put those early doubters in their place.

JOHN LENNON

In the 1950s, John Lennon's teacher wrote that he was 'certainly on the road to failure'. Yet Lennon and his friends Paul McCartney, George Harrison and Ringo Starr conquered the world as The Beatles, changing the face of popular music and impacting the entire world. John went on to release solo anthems and is without doubt a legend of British music.

ALBERT EINSTEIN

At the age of sixteen, the professor who revolutionised physics with his General Theory of Relativity was told by the head of his Munich school in a damning report that 'he will never amount to anything'. Yet Albert Einstein enjoyed a career showered with honours, including a Nobel Prize. Einstein later remarked philosophically, 'Great spirits have always encountered violent opposition from mediocre minds.'

The above are just a few examples of the many great people who could easily have had their careers utterly extinguished had they listened to the doubters, and if you search you will find hundreds if not thousands of other examples. Please consider that no other human being on the planet has the ability to know what you are capable of. With this in mind, we want you to live your life for you, and no matter what your dreams are, please know with absolute and utter confidence that any doubters should be disregarded entirely.

*

While you are now aware of the importance of disregarding the doubters you may encounter in your future, what about the doubters in your past who are having an effect on your life right now?

Have you listened to any doubters in the past and let their limits define you? If so, how many years ago was it that you allowed someone to tell you what you could or couldn't do in your life or what you were or were not capable of?

If most people look at how they are living their life today, it will be according to a set of schemas that they created in their past based upon other people's doubts. In our youth we often accepted opinions about what to believe, what we were capable of and who we were as a person, and those schemas then became invisible barriers that continue to control our lives in the present.

Nik remembers the circus coming to town during the school summer holidays, as it always used to set up in Royton Park, which was located at the back of his house. In fact, his bedroom overlooked the park and during the day he could see amazing exotic animals in the circus such as tigers, bears and zebras. The elephant was tied with a rope around its leg to a small stake in the ground, and Nik wondered why, as the biggest land animal, it didn't just pull the stake out of the ground and escape. Surely, it could do that with little or no effort at all? Nik knew the elephant had the strength to rip down the whole big top if it wanted to. He asked his dad why it didn't escape. He told him, 'Son, the elephant doesn't escape because he doesn't think he can – he has been conditioned that way. You see, they took him as a calf, and they put what then seemed to him a big rope around his ankle and attached it to what seemed to him to be a huge stake in the ground. The baby elephant then fought and fought to get loose from the stake, until one day he just decided he was not capable of pulling the stake out, and gave up.'

Had the elephant been a human, simply telling him about his limitations might have kept him attached to the stake. Once that schema was created, he gave up trying, as he believed his efforts would be futile. The elephant, a mammal just like a human, would carry on with the thought process, 'This is how it is, this is who I am, and therefore there is no point in ever trying again.'

Exercises

Your limiting schemas

We would urge you to take time to look at your limiting schemas. Even if they have been true in your past, ask yourself honestly: are they true now?

Were those limiting beliefs even your own limitations or imposed on you by others?

Were they based upon any evidence you had then? What about now?

When you have done this, make a list of your answers in the table opposite and ask yourself: what can I do right now to overcome these? If you are like that elephant, as soon as you realise that those limitations are nothing but a memory from the past and no longer apply, you can change the memory or condition it with new evidence, and this new realisation will help set you free.

Limiting schema	Was this belief mine or the result of someone else's influence on me? If so, whose?	What evidence do I have that my belief is incorrect?	What can I do right now to positively change this belief?
Examples: I can't apply for that promotion; I'll always be overweight; I'm not good-looking enough.	Example: My teacher told me I was stupid and would never amount to anything.	Examples: I have been headhunted; I have managed to lose weight in the past; my partner tells me I'm beautiful.	Example: I can remind myself of my successes in life.

(Table continued overleaf)

(Table continued)

Limiting schema	Was this belief mine or the result of someone else's influence on me? If so, whose?	What evidence do I have that my belief is incorrect?	What can I do right now to positively change this belief?

My supporters

Go through your mobile-phone contacts list and add an icon of a flexed bicep or smiley face to anyone who you perceive as someone who is positive, totally believes in you and champions you.

If in future you want any advice on anything you want to achieve or are contemplating doing, be sure to call and speak with those people (your igniters) only.

Friends

It really is great to have friends, and to belong to friendship circles that add depth and variety to our lives. Family members also become friends or through obligation feature regularly in our lives.

As we tend to like people who are similar to ourselves, we often adapt our behaviour around different friends, not because we are being insincere in any way, but because different friends and family bring out different traits in our personalities. For example, you may have friends who, when you are together, make you become animated, lively and fun. Conversely you will have some friends with whom you may have more serious discussions, and some with whom you just like a good gossip.

Having a wide variety of friends and acquaintances is great, but we can be in friendships that are thrust upon us out of obligation, such as with family members, work colleagues or partners of friends.

As the people we spend time with impact our mood, motivation, self-belief and drive, it is important to acknowledge which of the people around you ignite your positivity and self-belief, which do not and which could be considered doubters.

Friend	One word to describe this friend
Example: Susan	Examples: Positive, fun, doubter, negative, loyal

Completing this list will help you be aware of which friends will usually support your ideas and adventures – those you can feel safe sharing your hopes with. This list will also highlight who *not* to share your goals and dreams with until they are well under way, so that you can avoid any doubters stopping you in your tracks before you start.

Affirmations

'I am capable of achieving all my ambitions.
No other human has the ability to know what I am
capable of, nor have they the right to take any of my
ambitions away.'

'If it is possible in the world, it's possible for me!'

3

Accept Responsibility

Our third core schema is a big one: **accept responsibility**. We promise your life will change for the better when you do this.

You can go and see every counsellor in the world, talk to your friends for hours over endless cups of tea, read every self-help book available and travel the world looking for answers, but unless you put this knowledge into practice yourself, nothing will change.

It's very easy to hope that someone else will heal you, but no one can be by your side every moment of every day for the rest of your life. The only person who is with you 100 per cent of the time is you. And no one knows you, or will ever know you, better than you do.

Friends, family and relationships will come and go throughout your life, so the relationship you have with yourself should always remain the most important. Putting yourself first is not about being selfish – we want to make that very clear. In fact, it's all about being kind to others too, but we'll explain more about that later.

Self-preservation is about taking the best care of yourself that you possibly can, and the payoff is remarkable, not just for you but for everyone around you.

The moment you start to take full responsibility for your life is the moment when you can truly start shaping your dream future. Until you put the power into your own hands, you will always feel that your destiny is in the hands of others, and that can leave you feeling powerless. When we give our power to others, it's easy to become a part of someone else's goals instead of creating our own, so don't lose sight of the life upgrade that is yours, and yours alone.

When you take responsibility for yourself, you will find you're less negative. You can only be negative if you can justify to yourself and others that you are entitled to be angry, fearful or upset. You will notice that angry people are always justifying themselves and apportioning blame to others as to the reason for their negative feelings. Justification always requires that you make something or someone else the source of your problem, which in doing so renders you a victim of them or it. Equally, that also makes them or it your oppressor.

When we **accept responsibility** and begin to take positive action towards our goals, this negates the justification and excuses that promote our negative thoughts, feelings and emotions.

Continuing to justify negativity quite simply cultivates it and allows it to control you and your life. As soon as you **accept responsibility** to positively change your perspective and move on, the negative feelings will disappear and you will become a more positive and effective person.

Accepting Responsibility Will Set You Free

Accepting responsibility for your life may be particularly hard if you've grown up with controlling parents, been badly treated or have been in a relationship where your partner wanted to control you. These experiences can leave us questioning our own judgement and if they have happened to you, you may fall into a pattern of thinking that other people know what's best for you. But please believe us, no one knows what's better for you than you do. Don't feel bad if so far in life you have been swept along on someone else's

journey, because it's something that happen
population at one time or another. But acknov
power now is another step towards freedom.

The biggest part of taking back your power is
that you don't need to be a victim and blame other
for anything that happens to you. As soon as you do,   ∪u're
putting them in control of how you feel. If you can accept
that you've made mistakes, or that something that happened
to you wasn't personal, or if you can learn from a situation,
you can move on and release yourself to live your life.

Not letting go of past experiences is an anchor holding
you back from upgrading your life. When you carry around
all that hurt in an emotional rucksack it weighs heavily on
you. More heavily than you probably even realise. Imagine
that when you're born someone comes along and gives you
a nice, clean, empty rucksack to carry around. As you go
through life that rucksack gets filled with things that have
gone wrong, guilty feelings and things that have hurt you.
Unless you let them go, you'll feel bogged down, frustrated
and emotionally and physically exhausted from carrying your
heavy load. Think of the elderly people you see who walk
along with their shoulders hunched and their heads hanging
down as if they're carrying an invisible rucksack filled with
the weight of a lifetime's troubles.

Hatred is a heavy and toxic burden to carry that affects
you and only you. The recipient of your hate is oblivious
and experiences no repercussions whatsoever; the toxic
resentment hurts only you. An analogy that we feel is very
apt is that hatred is like you drinking poison and expecting
the other person or people to die. Bearing hatred for anyone,
no matter how much they may have wronged you, is totally
misguided as you are the only one who is affected.

Sadly, fault and responsibility are not the same. We know
that someone – and most likely more than one person – will
have hurt you and wronged you in your life, most probably

on more than one occasion, so please consider, if they have not turned up at your door and profusely apologised by now, they probably never will.

Consider this: it doesn't matter whose fault it is that something may be broken; if it's yours and you want to use it, then it's your responsibility to fix it. It's not your fault if your partner cheated on you and ruined your relationship. It certainly is, however, your responsibility to deal with that pain and look to how you can create a new life without them. Similarly, it's not your fault if you were brought up in a house of domestic violence. However, it is your responsibility to find a way to process any traumas from that upbringing, and to move forward with your life.

Do not lose sight of the fact that you – yes, you – are the master of your own fate. If you want to move forward in life, let go of hate and stop blaming others for what is, what was or what could have been. Blaming others is the worst response to pain and hurt, as it keeps us in the past and away from our future. Focusing on and complaining about things that happened in the past and cannot be changed only serves one purpose: it ensures that the past continues to hurt and punish you.

Accepting Responsibility Promotes Change

If you're struggling to see how accepting responsibility for mistakes and difficulties can help you move on, we get it. It's not always easy to put this one into practice when you're used to feeling stuck. So here are a few examples of famous names who took responsibility for difficult situations and were then able to move on.

ROBERT DOWNEY JR

Robert Downey Jr, who plays the iconic Marvel superhero character Iron Man, battled with addiction for many years. Although now a hugely respected Hollywood star, there was a time when he was considered un-hireable and too big a risk due to his drinking and drug use.

In 1996 he was arrested multiple times for bizarre and reckless behaviour, which included being stopped by police for speeding. He was found to be drunk and in possession of heroin, cocaine, and a .357 Magnum gun. On another occasion he actually walked into a neighbour's home and fell asleep in the neighbour's child's bed.

In 1999, after repeatedly missing court-ordered drug tests, he was sentenced to three years in prison. Robert Downey Jr admits that back then he had no desire to **accept responsibility** for his life, or any of the help being offered to him.

However, in 2003, Robert was cast alongside Halle Berry in the film *Gothika*, where he met his now wife, producer Susan Levin, and she gave him an ultimatum. She told him that she would leave him if he were to go back to drinking or taking drugs. Susan told him that it was time to **accept responsibility** for his life and get help.

Robert Downey Jr agreed, and because he accepted responsibility he has remained sober, and is still in a loving marriage with Susan while enjoying a successful career.

BILL CLINTON

Former US president Bill Clinton initially denied having sexual relations with his intern Monica Lewinsky back in 1998, and as a consequence there was an enormous backlash against him. His popularity plummeted and he was impeached (but acquitted).

However, as soon as Bill Clinton was honest and admitted what had happened between himself and Lewinsky, he was able to start rebuilding his career and regain his popularity. Some people even had a newfound respect for Bill.

Had he held his hands up from day one and admitted he'd made a mistake, he would have saved himself and his family an enormous amount of trouble, stress and upset.

HUGH GRANT

Hugh Grant is another great example of the power of accepting responsibility.

In 1995, he was in Los Angeles to promote his first major studio film, *Nine Months*, when he was arrested for committing a lewd act in a public place. The resulting media coverage saw him facing the loss of his career and his long-time girlfriend, and there was even the threat of a six-month prison sentence.

He could have made so many excuses. However, he took responsibility and said, 'I did something completely insane. I have hurt people I love and embarrassed people I work with. For both things I am more sorry than I can say.' Grant pleaded 'no contest' to the charges and was given two years' probation and a fine.

Shortly afterwards, he appeared on *The Tonight Show with Jay Leno* in a much-watched interview. When Leno asked him, 'What the hell were you thinking?' Grant answered, 'I think you know in life what's a good thing to do and what's a bad thing. I did a bad thing, and there you have it.' Grant was appreciated for his refreshing honesty, and his career, relationship and life stayed intact.

It's fine to make mistakes – we all do, because we're all human – and to be honest they are often a life lesson that helps develop our strength of character. However, the buck stops with you when it comes to being honest about them.

While not accepting responsibility, you are an antagonist. Whereas when you do **accept responsibility**, you become the solution. You can now draw a line in the sand and move forward knowing that you are, and forever will be, the captain of your ship.

Exercises

To start taking responsibility you must first make the decision that you will. Doing so can seem tough. However, without doubt it is a decision that will totally change your life.

Say it out loud

Many of our clients find it difficult to **accept responsibility**, and it's good to rehearse it internally before beginning to say it out loud. Taking ownership means being able to vocalise our feelings and intentions. These steps will help:

DAY ONE: In your head, say the words 'I am responsible for . . .' For example: 'I am responsible for my financial situation.' Even if you feel like your financial situation (or any other situation that you would like to change) is the result of other people's decisions or behaviour, take the responsibility yourself so you can make a positive change.

DAY TWO: When you are alone, say out loud, 'I am responsible for . . .' You may feel silly saying this out loud, but trust us. It's important to hear yourself say the words.

DAY THREE: To a close, trusted loved one, share with them the words 'I am responsible for . . .' It is a good idea to say this to someone who is separate from the difficult situation you are trying to change, someone who does not have anything at stake. That way they can hear you and support you rather than challenge you.

DAY FOUR: To friends and family you feel comfortable with, say, 'I am responsible for . . .' As above, choose friends and family who are going to be supportive and encouraging.

You will notice that it gets easier each day as the weight is lifted from your shoulders. Furthermore, vocalising your intent also makes you accountable and gives you an inner strength, all of which will help enable you to move on.

Taking responsibility

You now have the chance to upgrade your life by committing to accepting responsibility and choosing to change your perception of past events that have been holding you back.

We are not suggesting you take responsibility for anyone's actions or behaviours, nor any challenges or traumas you may have faced. Other people's unacceptable behaviour is not your fault, and you don't have to forgive it or them. We are, however, suggesting that you take responsibility for how you feel about old situations, traumas and people. Your feelings about everything are entirely within in your control.

We can't allow someone else's lack of apology to hold us back, so we have to let those feelings go. We can't change the past, but we can **accept responsibility** for how we choose to perceive it and we can finally cut those emotional ties and create a future that we want and deserve.

In this exercise we ask you to reflect in the table opposite on your life, the situations that have held you back, and the events and people that have stopped you from being the person you want and deserve to be.

I am taking responsibility for . . .	The first step I can take to improve this or my opinion of this is . . .
Examples: Being bullied by . . . ; being called names by . . . ; being made to feel inadequate by . . . ; being hurt by . . . ; being scared by . . . , etc.	Examples: Change my perspective by realising it wasn't personal to me/the bully was from an unstable home environment/they were envious of me/that person from my past no longer thinks about me/I was in the right place but at the wrong time, etc.

How you perceive yourself

We would also like you to take responsibility for how you perceive yourself, as most often our perception of ourselves as a person is based upon how other people have made us feel.

If you have been unfortunate enough to be in any abusive relationships, or surrounded by negative people in your life, particularly during your developmental years (from around the age of three to your early teens) then you are more likely to have negative self-belief or low self-worth. Again, please do bear in mind that these people who have been negative or unkind towards you have generally been brought up in a challenging environment or have been bullied or developed low self-esteem themselves. This in turn can make them envious of everyone and generally angry at the world. It is because of their personal issues that these people may have hurt you, said unpleasant things to you or made you feel bad about yourself.

We would now like to give you the opportunity in the table opposite to note how you perceive yourself, and to challenge anything that is negative.

Negative perceptions I have of myself	A more beneficial belief would be . . .
Examples: Worthless, shy, ugly, etc.	Examples: I add value to my family; I am learning to be confident; I am beautiful to the people who matter, etc.

My qualities

Now we would like you to list your positive qualities below (e.g. kind, compassionate, honest, loyal, thoughtful, trustworthy, intelligent, beautiful, fair). This can be difficult for some of us, so, if you're struggling, try to imagine how a loved one might describe you.

....

....

....

....

....

....

....

....

....

....

....

....

Friend criteria

Finally, we'd like you to consider what you expect from a good friend. Please list below everything that is important to you.

Our criteria for a good friend include (for example, honest, good listener, loyal . . .):

....

....

....

....

....

....

....

....

....

....

....

....

Now look at your 'Friend Criteria' list above and, hand on heart, ask yourself: do you have that quality? So, for example, if you wrote that your friend should be 'loyal', ask yourself the question, 'Am I loyal?' If the answer is yes, then place a tick at the side of that quality in your list and add these to your 'My Qualities' list.

What you should have noted from this exercise is that:

1. **You are unlikely to have noted anything about image or weight as a necessary requirement in a friend, so if you have image or self-esteem issues, you now have evidence here that how you look is neither relevant nor important to what matters in a friend.**

2. **You are likely to have ticked all or most of the 'friend criteria' you noted as important requirements in a good friend, which means you already fulfil your own best-friend criteria!**

Congratulations! It is now time to be your own best friend, as you now have proof you fulfil the attributes and qualities required.

Affirmation

'This is my life. I make my own choices and everything in my life is my responsibility.'

4

Anything
is Possible

Our fourth core schema is that **anything is possible** – yes, anything! Don't believe us? Well, you only need to look at the truly inspirational athletes of the Paralympics to know that this statement is true. One of the most amazing things we saw at the 2012 Paralympics when they were hosted in London was a high-jumper who only had one leg, but he didn't let it hold him back. It was literally breathtaking to watch him.

Some people may sustain a life-altering injury and have to use a wheelchair for the rest of their life, and as a result become incredibly unhappy and bitter. Yet other people faced with the same situation live a full and happy life, and even go on to win gold medals.

In the UK when you ask someone how they are, they quite often reply, 'Not so bad,' which would suggest that bad is the norm, and anything better than bad is OK. But that answer is also saying that they're not so good either, so pretty low actually. It's habitual for us to look on the downside of life because it's comfortable – if we don't say we're feeling great, we won't feel like we've let people down when we're not feeling that good anymore. So, we keep things on an even keel of 'OK' or 'not bad'. Should things go wrong, we're already prepared; however, this would also suggest we're constantly in a state of negative expectation!

When we think back to the Olympics and Paralympics hosted in London in 2012, we remember how, for the first time in years, there was a feeling of shared positivity in the air. Everyone seemed to feel that bit happier because they had something incredible to focus on. Instead of the usual British 'mustn't grumble' attitude, an optimistic unity developed. Suddenly there was a commonality between strangers, who were then able to chat like old friends about their shared passion for the sporting events. The same camaraderie was repeated in July 2021 when England made it through to the final of the UEFA Euro football championships. England had the chance of winning a major championship for the first time in fifty-five years and the feeling was electric. While they may have lost out to Italy in the final, it brought so much hope to the country and the belief that England could have a real chance of winning the World Cup again. Just imagine how many friends we could all have if we took the time to chat to a stranger on the bus or train and found an interest we had in common! We don't have to wait for an outside event to find common ground with strangers – we can make these connections at any time.

When we think about the schema **anything is possible**, we like to remind our clients that they don't have to reinvent the wheel. Instead, we suggest you look to successful people for inspiration. If you've always dreamed of becoming a runner, even just for a local team, but you keep making excuses not to do it, just think of all those athletes with prosthetic limbs who didn't let the fact that they didn't have two working legs hold them back.

There is always a way. Once you begin to believe in this and also to believe in yourself, you will find that way.

Society discourages us from telling other people how great we are, because that might be seen as big-headed or bragging, yet once this message seeps into our heads, we find it hard to tell ourselves how wonderful we are and how much we are capable of.

If you blow your own trumpet, you may be seen as arrogant, but why not celebrate how fabulous you are? For some reason it's fine for someone else to say how clever and talented you are, but if you say it about yourself, people think you're egotistical. Well, consider the fact that if you don't blow your own trumpet, then no one else is going to do it for you.

Nik likes to joke that there are many people who have a trumpet hidden away that needs to be taken out, dusted down and polished and then given a damned good blow, and often! Wake the world up to the fact that you're here, that you are amazing and you have accomplished some unbelievable things that you were told not to brag about. Get your trumpet and blow it as hard as you can!

Compliments

If someone gives us a compliment, we often think the right thing to do is to play it down or, even worse, disagree with it. When someone compliments us on an achievement, we say things like, 'It was just luck, really,' or, 'It's not that big a deal.' If you think about it, not accepting a compliment is actually unacceptable for the following reasons:

1. **You're suggesting that you don't believe what someone is saying – at worst, you might even be seen as calling them a liar!**

2. **You're diminishing your own achievements.**

3. **You're harming your self-worth by saying you don't deserve the compliment.**

It doesn't mean you have to reply, 'I know, aren't I just simply incredible?' when you are paid a compliment. But a simple 'thank you' goes a long way towards making your admirer glad that they made the comment. It will also help you believe that you deserve praise. Deflecting compliments is damaging to your self-esteem, whereas a simple 'thank you' helps to build it.

We believe that we're the world's leading inspirational life-change therapists. We don't say that because we're arrogant, we say it because we've worked incredibly hard for well over two decades to create ground-breaking therapies that work for people in a remarkably short space of time. By being confident in our abilities, we've helped to save many thousands of lives. If we believe in ourselves, other people will too, and they will be confident that we can help them. That's half the battle already won.

If people put us down for saying we're brilliant at what we do, we really don't mind because the positive benefit we receive from believing in ourselves is huge. We believe in ourselves, and that makes us happy. And we deserve to be happy. We all do. Everyone has a right to be happy, whether it's God-given or otherwise!

Look for Inspiration

If something is possible somewhere in the world, it's entirely possible for you too. You could liken success to making an amazing cake. Say someone spent thirty years of their life perfecting the most brilliant cake recipe and it worked wonderfully every time they used it. Out of kindness, they post their recipe on the internet and everyone else in the world starts following the recipe and getting the same amazing results immediately. Find the right recipes for your goals, and if they don't exist yet, don't be deterred – create them!

If you want to do something, find someone who has already successfully achieved it and look at how they made it work. If you follow their method, you will eventually obtain the same results. You may be faced with different challenges along the way and you may have to change course, but remember that failure only happens when you quit (see Chapter Five for more on this schema), as every action produces a result. If you don't get the result you wanted, you can still learn from it and become wiser; when you know what doesn't work, you can always try something different. Below are just a few people who have achieved the seemingly impossible:

JESSICA COX

There's an incredible lady called Jessica Cox who was born with no arms, yet she can do remarkable things such as drive a car and even put in contact lenses with her feet! She is currently the only person in the world with no arms who can fly a plane. Imagine how many people would have told her that was impossible. There are millions of people who would find the thought of flying a plane terrifying, let alone someone with that level of disability. She is living proof that **anything is possible**.

RICHARD BRANSON

Richard Branson is another incredibly inspirational figure. When he was a child his undiagnosed dyslexia meant he had a hard time academically, and this led to him dropping out of school. But he started his business the Virgin Group by using a phone box as his office and making people think he was a successful businessman. He has had no more breaks than anyone else and has got to where he is by sheer determination, belief and hard work. So, if your plan for the future is to become a billionaire entrepreneur, read as much as you can about Branson and others like him to get some tips.

SYLVESTER STALLONE

Sylvester Stallone was born with forceps and as a result his face was disfigured and his speech was slurred. When he grew up he decided that he wanted to be an actor, but he kept getting turned down for parts because they told him he couldn't speak properly. He got so low as a result of being rebuffed that he lost everything and was left with only his dog for company.

Inspired by a Muhammad Ali fight, and his own determination to succeed, Stallone wrote the script to a film he called *Rocky*.

Stallone then pitched *Rocky* to every film company going, until he found one person who offered to buy it from him for a lot of money. But the deal came with conditions – Stallone wouldn't be able to play Rocky. So, despite a good deal being on the table, he turned it down and walked out. He refused to compromise because his dream was to break into the acting industry by playing Rocky himself.

Finally he found a deal. It didn't pay much upfront as the deal was based on profit sharing, because the investors felt that having the unknown Stallone in the leading role was a massive risk. However, as we all know, the film went on to be a massive success worldwide, winning three Oscars.

When Stallone collected his award he read out some of the negative things that people had said about him. A lot of those people were reported to have been sitting in the audience that night and were no doubt kicking themselves. After *Rocky*, Stallone had some facial reconstruction surgery and went on to forge an incredible acting career. He went from being totally broke to being one of the most famous men in the world within a few years, simply because he refused to give up.

Follow Your Dreams

So many people really don't love their jobs; some view a job as nothing more than a way of getting paid and being able to sustain some sort of life, while some actively hate their job. However, now you know that **anything is possible**, if you are in a job you don't love then you must begin to follow your dreams after hours. If you work nine to five, then once your responsibilities are out of the way, you have to work on you, your brand and your better future, whatever that is.

Look back at your dream-life exercise (see pages 9–13) and work out the first steps towards your goals – then begin to take action.

There is a person, an idea, an adventure out there waiting for you to come and grab it with both hands.

Exercises

Read autobiographies and do research on the internet about people who have transformed their lives despite facing massive or even overwhelming odds. If you're not sure where to start, why not take a look at Zion Clark, a young man born with no legs, who was rejected by his mother, bullied, abused and moved around numerous foster homes, yet he is now a motivational speaker, author and champion athlete.

Think of ways you can apply other people's recipes for success to your own life. And be your own inspiration too – there will be so many things you have achieved in life, which at some point may have appeared unlikely, impossible or too difficult, yet you made them happen.

Often, as our achievements are progressive, we overlook the magnitude of what we have accomplished and how far we have come. For example, the first driving lesson you ever take is usually overwhelming when you suddenly realise that it's not as easy as it looks. Yet once you become a proficient driver, you forget to appreciate the magnitude of your achievement. Driving becomes something we take for granted, and we forget how much we have learned.

There are so many things you will have achieved, but due to progressive learning and experience you will have underestimated, taken for granted or forgotten the incredible journey you took to get there.

Consider that first day at work, yet now you are in a job you can carry out effortlessly. If you are a parent, you may recall the day your first child was born and thinking, 'How on earth will I manage this?' but you did it. Finally, how about those trips to the swimming pool when you needed armbands (water wings) or an inflatable ring to keep you afloat, yet now you can swim without either.

We would like you to note down your achievements in the list opposite and appreciate them. Consider all those things that once felt impossible but now feel easy, and applaud your successes – blow your own trumpet!

Remind yourself of things you have achieved, and of when you have been determined but thought you couldn't do something . . . yet YOU DID IT!

Write a list of A MINIMUM of ten life achievements. These can include passing an exam, succeeding at an audition or interview, falling in love, being a parent, an act of kindness, making someone laugh, consoling someone when they needed it, writing a letter, speaking out, standing up for yourself, giving a speech or learning to ride a bicycle, swim or play an instrument.

LIFE ACHIEVEMENTS

....

....

....

....

....

....

....

....

....

....

....

....

....

....

....

Affirmations

'Every little acorn has a strong oak tree within it.'

'If it's possible in the world, it's possible for me.'

'I can, I will, I know I can succeed!'

5

Failure Only Exists When You Quit

Our fifth core schema – **failure only exists when you quit** – may seem like a bold statement, but it's just about looking at things from another point of view.

Every time you attempt to do something you get a result, and that result gives you feedback. From that feedback you can decide if your action works or not. If it doesn't, you can try something else, so failure only exists if you stop trying something else.

So many people come to us and say, 'I've tried everything.' We know that if they had tried everything, they would have found the answer. If we then ask them to name ten things they've tried, which we usually do, they struggle to name even five because they've generally tried the same thing over and over again, even though deep down they know it doesn't work.

Try Something Different

Albert Einstein is supposed to have said, 'Insanity is doing the same thing over and over and expecting different results.' If the way you're doing things isn't working, learn from your failures and try a different way. Let failure be a stepping stone towards your goals. Here are some examples of famous people who did just that:

THOMAS EDISON

A fabulous example of the idea that there's no such thing as failure is Thomas Edison. It is reported that it took him over 10,000 attempts to invent the electric light bulb. Imagine if he had given up after 8,000 tries! His persistence led to an invention that completely turned the world on its head. Although Edison must have been hugely frustrated at times, he knew he was learning a huge amount and was getting closer to his goal with every step he took. He wasn't frightened of failure because he knew by failing he was actually getting ever closer to his goal of success.

JAMES DYSON

Another personal favourite of ours for inspiration is Sir James Dyson, the British inventor and billionaire entrepreneur who founded Dyson Ltd and invented the dual-cyclone bagless vacuum cleaner. Although Eva absolutely loves vacuuming, that is not the reason he is a personal favourite of ours – it's more due to his attitude and determination.

Dyson's belief in the idea of the cyclone vacuum cleaner was so important to him that, despite five years in production and 5,127 'failures', he never gave up. In 1983 he finally launched his G-Force cleaner. However, no manufacturer or distributor in the UK would get involved as they feared that the invention would negatively impact the market for replacement dust bags.

Undeterred, Dyson eventually launched his vacuum cleaner through a catalogue in Japan and the rest is history: his products are now available all over the world.

It's entirely possible to perceive yourself as a failure if it appears that not everyone in the world likes you, supports you or believes in you, so please remember this statement:

'I don't know the key to success, but the key to failure is trying to please everybody.' We live by that, because we know that you're searching for the impossible if you're trying to be liked by everyone around you.

If people think badly of us, we're the ones who are failing by letting them have any kind of negative effect on us. The bottom line is, not everyone in life is going to like you, no matter how hard you try. So if you want to succeed, stop trying to please others. That doesn't mean stop trying to be a good person, but do stop sacrificing your own happiness for others. If you are unhappy and unfulfilled, you won't be as well equipped to look after the people who truly matter and care about you.

You're not a failure if someone decides they don't want to be your friend. Some people are just more compatible than others. You don't have to be liked by everyone to be a success!

Insecurity

Sarah was chatting to her friend Jenny in the park when Jenny's friend Alice joined them. Alice and Sarah had never met before but were soon getting on really well. The moment Jenny mentioned that Sarah lived in London and worked in PR, Alice's attitude towards Sarah immediately changed. She made her excuses and left. Sarah was left feeling confused and assumed that she'd offended Alice. She wondered what on earth she had done wrong.

When Jenny later confronted Alice about her behaviour towards Sarah, she admitted that she felt insecure because Sarah was successful and glamorous, while she felt her own life as a housewife and mum was dull in comparison. She was embarrassed and felt like Sarah must have been looking down on her, which, in fact, couldn't have been further from the truth. The reality was that Sarah would have loved nothing more than to be able to meet someone and settle down herself.

The reality was that Sarah was envious of Alice, yet Alice's insecurities meant she interpreted the entire situation incorrectly.

Like so many of us, Alice thought she could predict what Sarah thought and felt. We all do this, and most of the time we are wrong! No one is a mind reader. People not getting along often has a lot to do with miscommunication or someone stirring up other people's insecurities. So, from today, remember that if someone seems to take umbrage at you, the likelihood is that it's more about them than it is about you. Don't jump to the wrong conclusion based on your initial assumptions.

We encountered a similar situation when we started appearing on TV and in the media. People we knew assumed we wouldn't want to be their friends anymore because in their eyes we were becoming 'celebrities'. They shied away from us without giving us a chance to show that we hadn't changed one bit and they meant as much to us as they always had. They made the decision for us that we'd changed because it stirred up negative emotions in them, whether it was jealousy, insecurity or simply feeling unsure of the relationship because of changes in our professional lives. Of course, we knew it wasn't about us as individuals because we were exactly the same as we'd always been.

FAILURE ONLY EXISTS WHEN YOU QUIT | 117

Exercise

Write a list of all the events in your life that you consider a failure in the table below, such as a past relationship, taking too long to achieve a certain task, not passing an exam or not getting a job you'd applied for.

Now, by the side of each one, write something positive that came from that failure. It could be something you learned or something you experienced or even someone new you met as a result of it . . . It may be just learning that you now know what not to do in the future, which could save you from repeating that failure.

Failure	Positive that came from that event
Example: Broke up with . . .	Example: Met a new person and started a better relationship.

(Table continued overleaf)

(Table continued)

Failure	Positive that came from that event

Affirmations

'There is always a solution to every problem.'

'If I haven't found the answer yet, I know I will, because when I start to look, I always find it.'

6

It's Never Too Late

Our sixth core schema is that **it's never too late**. This may sound like a crazy thing to say, but it's true. Look at Colonel Sanders, who set up KFC at the age of sixty-five, or Ray Kroc, who bought McDonald's at the age of fifty-two and turned it into a global franchise.

Another example (one that is closer to home) is the story of Eva's mum. Eva is going to tell this story because it's so personal to her.

EVA

My mum married my dad at the age of seventeen. They were married for almost forty years and my mum didn't have a career, so she came to be very dependent upon him. It appeared to me that Mum thought she was weak, worthless and couldn't live without him. She became unhappy in the marriage so I asked her why she stayed with my dad. She told me she was too fearful to leave because she had no idea how she would manage on her own financially. She had never had to stand on her own two feet in any way, so she was terrified of being alone.

The prospect of stepping out of her comfort zone was scary, but she had a few sessions with Nik and those sessions totally changed her outlook on life. They encouraged my mum to really put her life in perspective and to take on board our third core schema, **accept responsibility** (see Chapter Three), which allowed her to start taking control of her life.

Finally, my mum gained her confidence and the marriage ended. She was fifty-six when they divorced and now, at seventy-five, she holds a respected job, with her team begging her not to retire. She looks twenty years younger than her age, she owns property, and she found true unconditional love with a man younger than me who absolutely adores her! My mum is a fabulous, inspirational example of how **it's never too late** to change your life. She could still be immersed in her previous life, yet she has created this new magical life for herself, and she deserves every bit of it!

No Regrets

We once treated a lady aged eighty-two who suffered from emetophobia, which is an extreme fear of vomit, seeing other people be sick or even feeling sick. This might sound like a silly phobia, but her fear was restricting her life and preventing her from doing things she longed to do. At that age many people would just give up trying to find a way to sort it out and would accept their lot. Not this lady. She decided that enough was finally enough.

We successfully treated her and she's since been away on an amazing cruise, which she had dreamed of doing all her life. At least now, no matter what her future may hold or how old she is, she can say, 'I did it.' She will have no regrets.

The point is, no one cares how old you are when you decide the moment has finally arrived to change your life. The most important thing is that you're doing it. You may do some of the things you've dreamed of most in your older years because you had fears holding you back when you were young. Once you get over those stumbling blocks – and that's all they are – you could go on to create some of your greatest memories.

We've spoken to many senior citizens in their eighties and older. They all agree that they have no regrets about the things they've done in their life, but they do regret the things they wanted to do but never attempted. It's vital, therefore, not to put age restrictions on yourself. Live an eventful life by creating it right now, no matter what your age.

Some of the world's biggest success stories didn't get to where they wanted to be until they were in their forties, fifties, sixties and older, because they weren't yet ready. Below are just a couple of examples.

CAITLYN JENNER

Someone who proved it really is never too late to be the person you are meant to be is American media personality, world-record holder and retired Olympic gold-medal-winning decathlete Caitlyn Jenner.

Born William Bruce Jenner, at the age of sixty-six, Caitlyn publicly came out as a transgender woman. Although she had known her true gender identity all her life, she had kept it secret and used the frustration and confusion she felt within her to train as a decathlete.

After three marriages and six children, and with a very successful television presence, Caitlyn made the brave step to finally be who she was supposed to be. At the age of sixty-eight, Caitlyn completed sex reassignment and has gone on to inspire many thousands of other transgender people all around the word who had previously chosen to hide away.

E.L. JAMES

E.L. James wanted to write a book her entire life but doubt and a lack of confidence blocked her from taking action. However, once she shifted those blocks and the time felt right, she went for it and her book, *Fifty Shades of Grey*, became a global sensation. E.L. James became a multi-millionaire at the age of forty-eight.

Just because you don't feel like you can do something right now does not mean you can never do it. Always keep in mind the old and very true saying: 'Age is nothing but a number!'

Exercises

Think yourself young

You become what you think about, therefore think of yourself with the energy and optimism of your teenage years. Put on some music from your youth, have a dance and allow yourself to step into your younger self as a reminder of the energy, excitement and enthusiasm you once had.

If you've done something before, you can do it again. Reignite the youthfulness within yourself by carrying out this exercise frequently, listening to music from your younger years in your car, at home or on your phone.

Your last day on earth

To ensure you do not overlook your goals, dreams and desires, we'd like you to note down in the following list anything you would regret if today were your last day on earth . . .

Never having seen . . .

....

....

....

....

....

....

Never having said . . .

....

....

....

....

....

....

Never having visited . . .

....

....

....

....

....

....

Never having tried . . .

....

....

....

....

....

....

....

Never having tasted . . .

....

....

....

....

....

....

....

Never having experienced . . .

....

....

....

....

....

....

....

Never having read . . .

....

....

....

....

....

....

Never having learned . . .

....

....

....

....

....

....

Never having watched . . .

....

....

....

....

....

....

....

Affirmations

'The older I become, the more wisdom I acquire to help me achieve my dreams.'

'Aging? That's just another word for living.'

'Getting old is mandatory; fortunately growing up isn't.'

7

Plan
Your Life

Our seventh core schema is to **plan your life**. It sounds so simple, yet very few of us take steps to really plan how to achieve our dreams and upgrade our lives.

In order to change your life, you need to know what you want out of it. For example, if you go supermarket shopping with a list, you invariably come out with exactly what you went in there for. However, if you don't make a list, the chances are you'll forget the main items you went in for and will come out with a load of stuff you didn't really want.

Life is like a supermarket full of distracting choices. Essentials like potatoes, bread and eggs are purposely set far apart so you have to go down aisles laden with far more tempting goods in order to get the things you really want. Hence you come out with things you didn't actually need.

Life is the same: unless you sit down and **plan your life**, instead of it progressing in the way you want it to, you're going to end up weighed down with things you never really wanted, having exhausted yourself by tramping up and down the aisles of life, not really getting what you dream of or actually deserve. The likelihood is that on some level, no matter how deep, you already know what you really want.

A great analogy for planning your life is imagining you've got a pair of blue shoes and a pair of red ones, and you ask someone which colour you should wear. You do already know the answer yourself. However, you're simply asking someone else to confirm your choice. If that person tells you to wear the blue shoes when you wanted to wear the red ones, you'll feel unhappy about it all day because you'd made the decision before you even posed the question. However, perhaps due to a fear of judgement or low self-esteem, you are seeking validation. In essence, you are compromising your happiness by listening to other people's opinions, despite those people not necessarily sharing your life experiences, thoughts and desires, or having any qualifications in fashion.

The knowledge of what you want, and what is best for you, is already inside you. Therefore, if you listen to someone else and then wear the blue shoes, the chances are you're going to feel resentful and wish you'd gone with your gut feeling at the outset.

A good example of already having the answers involves James, a workman we know. He had been having some problems with his wife. They'd been arguing a lot and he thought the relationship could be over. He talked to us about it in some detail and told us he'd been taking advice from his brothers and a friend, all of whom thought he should leave the marriage. We asked about the relationship status of his advisors, and it turned out that one brother had never married, while the other had just got divorced after an unhappy relationship. Meanwhile, his friend was in a relationship but was cheating on his girlfriend.

We asked James to tell us about his parents' marital situation, to which he replied that they had been happily married for just over fifty years. So we asked him what his parents, after all those years of marriage, had to say on the matter. He didn't know as he hadn't asked them. It was only at that moment that he realised his parents were the best equipped to give him advice, because deep down he wanted to work on his relationship, just as they had worked on their own for over fifty years.

James was being distracted from his own gut instinct by the advice of three people, all of whose relationships were ones he wouldn't choose for himself. He realised that he was finding their advice confusing because it didn't match his desire to work on his marriage.

The truth is, our gut instinct is usually right, but we doubt ourselves due to our schemas, which may be based on situations such as being told off at school for making a mistake or answering a question incorrectly in class and everyone laughing. When we don't acknowledge and positively challenge these events with an alternative perspective, such as 'making mistakes helped me to learn' or 'it was brave of me to offer an answer in class, even if it was incorrect', then these schemas continue to play into our subconscious.

You Know Best

Most people, on an unconscious level, don't trust their decisions or their own instincts even though more often than not they have the answers, and know what they really do want from their life. If we have been taught at school or by our family how we should think, act or feel, we can become indecisive because we have learned to question our own judgement.

The clearer we are about what we want and the more focused we are on our dreams, the more likely they are to happen. So learn to listen to yourself and what you want from your life. No matter how much advice other people try to give you, go with your gut instinct and make your plans accordingly. Here's a very famous example of someone who did just that:

ARNOLD SCHWARZENEGGER

Arnold Schwarzenegger is a great example of someone who went with his instincts, planned his life and achieved goals that once felt far out of reach.

Arnold's goal was always to become a movie actor in America. He realised that in order to do that he had to accomplish something big to make an impact, but he had no idea how. One day, while in a sports shop, he saw bodybuilder Reg Park on the cover of a magazine. Arnold learned that Reg had won Mr Universe three times and as result he had become an actor, starring as Hercules. Arnold saw his path to the movies clearly from that moment, believing he could do it too.

No one else bought into his idea. In fact, his parents thought he was insane. He had pictures of Reg Park in his bedroom for inspiration so he could see them last thing at night and first thing in the morning, and as a result his mother called the local doctor and had him analyse Arnold's bedroom wall, as she thought there might be something terribly wrong with him. She couldn't understand why he had pictures of semi-naked men on his bedroom walls, whereas all his friends had posters of female popstars.

At the age of twenty Arnold became the youngest Mr Universe ever, beating Reg Park's record by four years. Six years after setting his goal, he was invited to America, where he was told to change his name if he wanted to become a successful actor. He ignored the advice and became a hugely successful Hollywood star and a household name regardless.

What we really like about Arnie is how honest he is in his autobiography. Some successful people make out that their life is a magical fairy tale that happened without them having to put in any effort. It's as though they were just born brilliant! Arnie is totally honest about the fact that in following his dreams he set clear goals and left nothing to chance.

The Reticular Activating System

No matter how ridiculous or far out of your reach something may seem, it can all be grasped once you engage something called the reticular activating system (RAS), which is a network of neurons located at the stem of your brain.

The RAS is like a radar for all the things that we tell it are important to us. You'll be aware of your RAS being activated if you've ever thought about buying a car. Once you identify the make and model that you're interested in, you suddenly seem to see these cars everywhere! You think, 'How did that happen? I hardly ever saw any of these cars on the road before.' Those cars were always there, but your reticular activating system now sees them because they've become important to you.

A personal example of RAS that really makes us smile is when a man walked into our fitness club in 2002 looking to join. He asked how it was all going with the club, and when we replied that it was going really well, that we'd been open for four years and each year had been better than the one before, he said, 'That's impossible, you've only been open for about two weeks!' He lived on the same road as the club and had walked past it every day going to and from work, but he had only noticed the club for the first time when he'd decided he needed to get in shape. His reticular activating system had noticed the club the very next time he passed by.

Some years ago, we worked with a gentleman who, although he was a life coach, didn't feel entirely fulfilled by his life. We worked with him to help him discover things that he'd dreamed of but hadn't achieved or even considered for many years. After putting together a life plan, he went on to tell us that he was desperate to go up in a hot-air balloon. The next time we saw him, he'd done exactly that. He said to us, 'You won't believe what happened. After I saw you, I went home and while reading my local paper there was an advert for hot-air balloon rides. How weird is that? Talk about a coincidence.' That was no coincidence!

Was that the first time that advert had been in that newspaper? No, it had probably been in there every week, but he hadn't registered the article until he had engaged his reticular activating system. By telling himself that hot-air ballooning was now important to his life, his RAS picked up on the advert at that particular time, simply because it was now relevant to him.

A lot of people believe in coincidences or think they're psychic because they'll think of something and then they'll see it, but it's only because their RAS has been engaged and is actively looking for it. It's just like an in-built radar system, which just needs to be switched on and directed in the right way.

So once you identify your goals and dreams and plan for them, your RAS will activate and help you see opportunities that you may have overlooked many times before.

Most people don't even think about planning their life. They get up in the morning, they go to work, they come home and they go to bed. Then they get up and do it all again. They think having a good life relies on whether their boss decides to promote them or whether or not they get a pay rise. They're giving other people power over their lives because they're not making a plan. If you want that pay rise, you need to plan it into your life and make it happen.

So many people live their lives like leaves blowing in the wind. They might blow to a nice area and have a house and some kids, but they may blow to a place they don't like and never meet a partner and end up miserable. People don't realise just how in charge of their lives they really are.

Think about ships, in the days before engines. Although the wind would be blowing in many different directions, the ship had a destination to reach. By adjusting the sails with each wind change they would always reach their destination, as opposed to going only where the wind took them. In modern times you could have the best, most opulent cruise ship in the world, but if your captain doesn't have a clear destination, they, you and everyone on the ship would just end up drifting around.

We love working with people to help them discover exactly what they want from life and how to get it. We remember one man saying that part of his life plan was to be wealthy enough to have a Bentley. One day he rang us out of the blue to say he wanted us to be the first people to know that he was just about to drive his brand-new Bentley out of the showroom. Amazing things can and do happen.

We don't believe in random luck. The harder you work, the luckier you get, as luck happens when preparation meets opportunity. People may say that someone who's gone on a television talent show and landed a record deal is lucky, but that's not down to luck. Before they even went on the show they planned to be a singer, and they may have played gigs in every small venue in the country beforehand. They also had to take action and go to auditions, plan their song choices, decide what they would wear and be prepared to work incredibly hard. It's not just by chance that they've ended up there.

Other people may have similar ambitions to be a singer but can't be bothered to get up at 5 a.m. and travel to the auditions. They don't want to spend money on a new outfit and the thought of all the work that comes with being famous feels too exhausting. They have the dream, but not the plan to achieve it.

We think the best way to get started is to create a plan for your life so big that it makes you feel a bit uncomfortable! Aim big, and then to keep yourself motivated and negate the feeling of overwhelm, concentrate on one small part of the plan at a time. If you had to climb a mile-long staircase, the thought of reaching the top might be really exciting, but when you reach the bottom of the staircase, the sight of a mile of stairs might put you off even getting started. But you don't have to climb the whole staircase straight away; all you have to do is concentrate on climbing one step – that's all. No matter how long it takes you, once you climb that first step you can then focus on the next step, and so on.

You have the power to create everything that happens in your life. We quite simply cannot say that often enough!

Exercises

Write yourself a life plan of everything you want to achieve. You need a very clear vision of where you want to go, and only then can you get there. Here are some examples of how you can plan various parts of your life.

Perfect partner

If part of your plan is to meet a perfect partner then write down all of the attributes you want that partner to have. Be specific. It may sound cold but it's absolutely not. Imagine you're designing your perfect partner and include everything from their looks, hobbies and career to their religious views, politics, morals and values.

Writing down all these components will help you to look in the right places for what you want. For example, if you are looking for the perfect partner and you want someone who enjoys sport and a healthy lifestyle, you're unlikely to find them in a fast-food restaurant.

Once you've written your list, narrow it down to a list of the top ten most important items to focus on, then look over your list often and your reticular activation system will do the rest.

Perfect Life Plan

Before embarking on designing your life below, reread the exercise you completed in 'Your Personal-life Upgrade' at the start of this book, where you noted down what your perfect life would look like (see pages 9–13). Also reread 'Your last day on earth' exercises at the end of Chapter Six (see pages 126–31). All the things you wrote down there can be added to your life plan list below.

It is important when writing your list that you imagine you are living in a world where **anything is possible** (see Chapter Four). Where money, age, qualifications and abilities are all irrelevant and not a necessity.

To **plan your life**, write a list of everything you've ever wanted to do, see, be or experience. Include career, home, cars, holidays, hobbies, charities, qualifications and anything and everything you've ever wished for, dreamed of, aspired to be or would regret if you never experienced or tried it.

Have fun with this – it's like a magic wish list!

MY FUTURE

....

....

....

....

....

....

....

....

....

....

....

....

The best way to predict your future is to create it.

Now you have your list, we'd like you to put a number alongside each goal to indicate when you'd like to achieve it by:

1   **To signify that you would like to achieve this goal within one day to one year.**

3   **To signify that you would like to achieve this goal within three years.**

5   **To signify that you would like to achieve this goal within five years.**

10   **To signify that you would like to achieve this goal within ten years.**

10+   **To signify that you would like to achieve this goal in over ten years.**

You can now separate your goals and write them on the following pages, adding your one-year goals to the one-year list, your three-year goals to the three-year list, your five-year goals to the five-year list, and so on.

Usually, people find that most of those they have written down are one-year goals.

WITHIN ONE YEAR

....

....

....

....

....

....

....

....

....

....

....

> *Do something today that your future self will thank you for.*

WITHIN THREE YEARS

....

....

....

....

....

....

....

....

....

....

....

....

> *Regardless of your past, your future is a clean slate.*

WITHIN FIVE YEARS

....

....

....

....

....

....

....

....

....

....

....

....

You miss 100 per cent of the shots you don't take.

WITHIN TEN YEARS

....

....

....

....

....

....

....

....

....

....

....

....

A little progress each day adds up to big results.

OVER TEN YEARS

....

....

....

....

....

....

....

....

....

....

....

....

The key to success is to focus on goals, not obstacles.

Now, from your 'Within 1 Year' list, choose three one-year goals you would like to start working on immediately.

Write one goal in each section below and then add one small action you can take to make each of these goals a reality. The step does not have to be huge; it can be as small as making a telephone call, asking a question or researching online. Once you start with the first step, the second should naturally follow and the actions required to attain your goal will start to gain momentum.

GOAL 1

....

....

....

....

GOAL 2

....

....

....

....

GOAL 3

....

....

....

....

We suggest you use a diary in conjunction with your goals list, so you can plan your steps. For example, if you set a goal in January of running the London Marathon, but the applications are not accepted until August, then you'll want to put a note in your diary that the application date is in August. Once this is in your diary, a new one-year goal from the list is then brought forward for action.

Be sure to read and reflect on your goals often. By doing so, you will see opportunities you may have missed before and this will keep your reticular activating system on high alert, looking for new opportunities. Start working on your next goal as soon as you have completed one or have noted a prompt in your diary for the next step of a goal that may be time sensitive.

Don't forget to celebrate when you achieve your goal, and set small rewards for yourself along the way too. For example, if running a marathon is your goal, celebrate during your training when you are able to run five miles, then ten miles, etc.

Reflect fully on all your goals annually, and add to, renew or replenish them at the start of each year. We set our new goals each New Year's Day. We and our children write down our individual goals and then together we create family goals as well for the year ahead.

We are so thrilled for you as we know that by setting goals, and taking action towards completing them, you have many exciting new adventures, experiences and achievements ahead of you.

Affirmations

'I plan my own life goals, so that I don't become a part of someone else's plan.'

'It's my life and I will live it as I want!'

'I will turn my dreams into my goals.'

8

You Are
What You Eat

Our eighth core schema is a phrase you will have heard often before: **you are what you eat**. As common as this expression is, we find that very few people actually respond to its powerful message or really take on board the simplicity of its words.

Your body is a vehicle that drives you through life. Like a car, your body needs fuel to run efficiently, for energy, for your organs to work well, for your cells to regenerate, for your hair and nails to grow and, most importantly, to keep you healthy and able to fight disease.

If you add poor or polluted fuel to your car, it will run poorly, you will have a bumpy journey, parts will fail – or worse, the car could stop working altogether. Your body is not really any different. The simple fact is that poor, polluted fuel or food will stop your body running efficiently. Poor food causes illness, disease, lethargy and ultimately death. Obesity, diabetes, strokes, heart disease and cancer are just a few of the diseases that have become more prevalent in today's society, and they appear to have increased at the same rate as the growth and popularity of fast-food outlets, ultra-processed foods, high-sugar diets and dairy consumption.

We have this core schema because it is a simple truth that if you eat poorly, you will feel poorly, and this will have a negative impact on your life. Conversely, if you eat well, you will feel well, and this will have a positive impact on your life. It really is that simple and yet millions of people in the world are either oblivious to this or choose to overlook such an obvious way to feel better and happier. Right now, please just take a few moments to really consider how eating well, continually feeling well and having more energy will allow you to improve all aspects of your life.

We understand that transitioning to eating healthier foods can take time, but you don't have to do it overnight! In fact, drastic dietary or lifestyle changes are rarely sustainable, whereas small weekly changes over a year can totally transform your diet and your life.

When Nik was given the prognosis of having only weeks to live, this core schema – **you are what you eat** – saved his life. We know from experience that understanding this schema, and putting it into action, can literally make the difference between life and death.

When we met, Eva was a big dairy fan, and as a vegetarian her diet consisted of a significant quantity of cheese, yoghurt and milky drinks. She suffered from irritable bowel syndrome (IBS), with a combination of symptoms from bloating and urgency to use the toilet to constipation or diarrhoea. IBS-type symptoms can also be created by the over-production of adrenaline, and having a home life with a significant level of anxiety also contributed to her condition. However, after Nik shared his negative experience with dairy products, she also stopped consuming them and was really shocked at how quickly the IBS symptoms and bloating disappeared altogether.

Consider cutting out dairy

Without wanting to make this chapter solely about dairy, suffice it to say we are a totally non-dairy yet very healthy household, consuming only almond, oat, coconut and more recently pea milk.

Together we have studied the effects of cows' milk, which is obviously specifically produced for a calf, to take that calf of approximately 63lb at birth to a fully grown cow of between 900lb and 1,500lb over a period of only two years. Coupled with the hormones, antibiotics and growth hormones that dairy cows are given, this is not a great combination for humans, who take up to twenty years to grow to their full size and on average nowhere near the weight of a cow.

Interestingly, we are the only animal on the planet that drinks another animal's breast milk. Many people feel repulsed at the thought of drinking a cup of tea made with human breast milk, yet we don't hesitate to ingest liquid excreted from a cow's udders. Many cows suffer regularly from mastitis and crusty, infected nipples from the harsh metal suckers that extract their milk usually twice daily. This leads to cows being pumped with antibiotics and hormones, which can then be transmitted to the milk that humans drink.

Interestingly, at the time of writing, China, which until recently did not have a dairy industry, does not appear among the fifty countries with the highest levels of cancer. Although these findings may appear coincidental or somewhat controversial, the Western world has slowly started to realise the negative effects of dairy, and as such a whole host of alternatives have appeared in supermarkets, such as soya milk, rice milk, coconut milk, almond milk, cashew milk, hazelnut milk, oat milk and pea milk.

Why not try a dairy-free experiment for a few weeks and see if you notice any changes in your health or mood?

Avoid ultra-processed foods

Ultra-processed food such as ready-meals, processed meats, cakes, biscuits and fried snacks are manufactured using multiple ingredients combined with additives and flavoured with sugar, salt, fats and chemical preservatives. Although they may be convenient and taste good, the truth is that ultra-processed foods offer no health benefits.

While it's acceptable to have a little processed food in moderation from time to time, we do have to **accept responsibility** for the fuel we choose to consume and the quality of that fuel. Recent studies suggest that for every 10-per-cent increase in the amount of processed food we eat, there could be a 14-per-cent higher risk of early death.[1]

We tend to turn to ultra-processed food because it is quick and convenient, and therefore it is important to plan meals for the week ahead and cut down on purchasing ultra-processed food where we can. Why not take advantage of online shopping, so you can have healthy food delivered directly to your door, saving you from having nothing to eat but ready-meals? Poor-quality food will offer you a poor quality of health and wellbeing, and you and your body deserve better.

Can you set yourself a goal to cut ultra-processed food right down? Perhaps start with one day where you don't eat any processed foods. And then you may feel inspired to expand this to two days, three or more.

Take a probiotic

When looking for a solution to improving his gut health, Nik became aware of probiotics. Due to consistently being on antibiotics throughout his childhood, he had traumatised his gut microbiome, and having taken probiotics for forty years now, Nik would never be without them. Rather excitingly, a lot of research has now been conducted regarding the brain–gut axis, into the theory that changes in gut bacteria can also have a positive impact on neuropsychiatric conditions such as anxiety and depression. Reviews of numerous psychological research studies in this area have shown probiotics to have positive effects on these mental-health conditions and suggest a very promising outcome for the potential future use of probiotics alongside, or even instead of, routine antidepressant medications.[2]

The reason for these beneficial mental-health effects of probiotics is likely the consequent reduction in cortisol – a hormone involved in the human stress response – the potential reduction of neuroinflammation in the brain and the resulting boost in 'feel-good' neurotransmitters, such as serotonin.

Serotonin is perhaps the most well-known chemical for affecting moods, and many people suffering with depression are often diagnosed with low serotonin or a chemical imbalance. Few people, however, seem to be aware that up to 90 per cent of our serotonin is created in our gut![3] When you consider this fact alone, it becomes clear that looking at the foods you eat and looking after your gut can help you subsequently look after your brain better – and make your *feel* better in the process!

Keep hydrated

If we didn't oil our car engines, they would run poorly and eventually seize up. Your body is no different and hydration is paramount to your health and wellbeing.

Drinking water has many benefits, which include cleansing your body and skin, speeding up your metabolism, aiding in the removal of waste, offering an appetite suppressant and even reducing puffiness and water retention in the body.

When we realised the health benefits of being properly hydrated, we had to train ourselves to drink more water, as it wasn't a habit of ours. We did this by drinking a pint of water in the morning on waking, and then would not allow ourselves to drink our usual daytime drinks of tea or coffee unless we drank a pint of water first. Although at first you will notice that your need to urinate is accelerated, this is a great sign that your body is removing toxins and water retention, as it no longer needs to hold onto water.

Once you train your body in the benefits of being well hydrated, you will actually find yourself wanting to drink water, and the habit becomes easier. In our experience, the best formula for how much water to drink as an individual is a minimum of 0.6fl oz for each pound you weigh each day.

Cut down on alcohol

Everything in moderation is acceptable, so we are not being party poopers when we point out that limiting alcohol will help you upgrade your physical and mental wellbeing.

Alcohol is a chemical. Not only can it be detrimental to our organs and increase the probability of illnesses such as cancer, but it also interferes with the brain's communication pathways. Alcohol can lower our mood and make us behave in ways that, when sober, can cause a lot of sadness and regret.

Furthermore, alcohol is not only calorie heavy, it can also make us eat more, interfering with our sober good intentions and sparking a new pattern of overeating.

We'd suggest starting by having two or three alcohol-free days a week. Notice your mood on those days when you don't drink, and the days afterward. Alcohol is a depressant, and many people find their mood lifts when they drink less.

Limit sugar

There is a lot of evidence out there that sugar is damaging to our health and contributing to an epidemic of type 2 diabetes in the Western world. A healthy diet can incorporate some sugar, but pay attention if you are using sugar for energy or as comfort food.

Sugar raises your blood sugar, which gives you a temporary high, but then it makes your blood sugar crash to a very low point, which makes you crave more sugar than before. Have you ever noticed how it's hard to eat just one biscuit? That's your blood-sugar crash urging you to eat more. Try to limit your sweet treats to mealtimes and avoid eating sugar on an empty stomach.

Why not try a few sugar-free days a week and see if it makes a difference to how you feel?

Reduce gluten

Gluten is predominately found in foods such as bread, pasta, cakes, pizza and biscuits. It is a gluey plant protein, which has no nutritional value but is used to glue or bind ingredients together.

While gluten is known to be an antagonist of symptoms for people with celiac disease, many people are actually sensitive to gluten, with some not realising their bloating, wind, stomach cramps, constipation and diarrhea could be due to gluten sensitivity. Gluten has been tied to irritable bowel syndrome (IBS) and other bowel inflammatory disorders such as Crohn's Disease and ulcerative colitis, and to adversely affect the positive benefits of gut bacteria.

Nourish your body

Happiness does come from within, and we have no doubt that you already know that a healthy mind and a healthy body go hand in hand.

The equation to a heathy body is simply: exercise + hydration + a healthy diet.

There are no better nutrients for your body than raw natural foods, such as nuts, fruit and vegetables. These foods are a natural energy source, jam-packed with beneficial fats, fibre to keep you feeling full for longer and to promote healthy bowels, and vitamins and minerals to nourish your body, keep it healthy and help your body to run efficiently and energetically.

Furthermore, natural and raw fruit and vegetables are low in sodium so help to avoid conditions such as stroke, high blood pressure, heart conditions, osteoporosis, some cancers and type 2 diabetes.

The great thing about these natural foods is that you can eat them without restriction and know that in doing so you are helping your body.

We have researched and discovered many examples of people whose health has improved as a result of introducing raw natural foods to their diet and removing dairy. We have also come across a number of cases of people being told they were terminally ill, only to regain full health following the removal of dairy from their diet and increasing consumption of raw natural vegan foods.

One such gentleman was a seventy-eight-year-old grandfather called Allan Taylor who in 2012 was diagnosed with terminal colon cancer, yet within four months of changing his diet, he was given the all-clear.[4] Allan replaced meat and dairy with ten pieces of fruit and vegetables each day. He also incorporated powdered wheatgrass, curry spices, apricot seeds and selenium tablets into his diet. Allan is just one of many we have come across who has felt the benefits of natural nourishment.

If you'd like to take the advice above to the next level, why not spend the next two weeks avoiding all dairy, sugar, gluten and ultra-processed foods and note how you feel? Be careful of milk derivatives that are hidden in processed foods that you would not expect.

As well as noting your mood and energy levels, take some 'before' and 'after' photos and measurements of your stomach and waist, and a side-on photo of your tummy so you can observe any reduction in bloating. Also take photos of your hair and skin and note the difference after six weeks free from dairy, sugar, processed foods, gluten, etc. and with the addition of fruit, vegetables and more water. Be sure to speak with your GP if you have any health conditions that may be affected by removing gluten from your diet.

Take More Exercise

The benefits we reap from regular exercise, movement and activity is abundant. Exercise enhances our physical and mental health, and offers increased mobility, energy and self-confidence.

Benefits of exercise include:

- **Weight control**

- **Reduced risk of heart disease, type 2 diabetes, high blood pressure, anxiety, depression, stroke and arthritis**

- **Increased energy, strength, confidence and mobility**

- **Can be a good way to make friends and extend your social circle**

- **Can improve sleeping patterns**

- **Generally promotes better health**

You don't have to join a gym or take part in a public aerobics class to move more. A regular brisk walk outside, dancing in your kitchen or even vacuuming or cleaning all constitute movement, so exercise can be free and readily available to all.

Consider Your Choices

No one eats food by mistake. Whether we eat something
healthy or something not so nutritious, it is always based
on a choice. It is easy to snack or pick at things and then
either conveniently forget or ignore what we have actually
consumed.

To make unacceptable situations acceptable, we can on
occasion be dishonest with ourselves or forget to note just
how much we have really eaten to lessen our feelings of guilt
or regret. A great first step to improving your eating habits is
to first acknowledge your accurate eating patterns and food
intake by completing the food diary overleaf for two weeks
to document everything you eat. This will also allow you to
notice any patterns when you feel energised or sluggish,
giving you clues and allowing you to identify the foods that
give you more energy or, conversely, those that make you
feel lethargic.

Be sure to keep this book with you so you can note down
literally everything that you eat, snack on, drink or even just
nibble on while cooking.

My food diary

WEEK 1	Breakfast	Lunch
Monday		
Tuesday		
Wednesday		
Thursday		
Friday		
Saturday		
Sunday		

Dinner	Snacks	Alcohol

WEEK 2	Breakfast	Lunch
Monday		
Tuesday		
Wednesday		
Thursday		
Friday		
Saturday		
Sunday		

Dinner	Snacks	Alcohol

You can continue to complete and keep a food diary for longer than two weeks if you wish, which can really help you structure and take control of your eating. Also, having to write it down makes you accountable and therefore less likely to overindulge. However, a great benefit of this food diary is to help you look at the food groups you indulge in the most, and those you do not have enough of, to ensure a healthy, balanced diet.

You can use different-coloured highlighters to give a clearer indication of the food groups you are eating that you should avoid or reduce to give you the healthiest outlook possible.

For example:

- **Dairy (such as butter, cream, yoghurt, milk or cheese) – highlight in yellow**

- **Sugar (simple sugars such as those in cakes, sweets and chocolate) – highlight in pink**

- **Alcohol – highlight in green**

- **Ultra-processed foods – highlight in orange**

With this information you can now start to look at healthier substitutes and alternatives, and decide what to omit from your shopping list to prevent temptation.

Our bestselling book *Winning at Weight Loss* can give you a great understanding of the causes of your overeating and offers solutions, helping to change your perception of and relationship with food. If this is an area that you need help with, reading our book could be something you may wish to add to your list of one-year goals (see page 146).

Affirmations

'I am what I eat, so I eat healthy food to be healthy.'

'Health is the real wealth.'

'A healthy outside starts with a healthy inside.'

9

Save Yourself Before You Save the World

Our ninth core schema may sound like a selfish one: **save yourself before you save the world**. But we'll demonstrate in this chapter how being good to yourself makes it easier for you to do good for others.

To a certain extent we are all people pleasers, so we will often do more for other people than we will to look after ourselves. However, if you spend your life looking after your husband or wife, children and friends, but you don't look after yourself, you could end up getting ill and then not being able to look after anyone, including yourself. And that, ultimately, is a burden on those you love. If you put aside time for yourself to go to the gym, or to practise mindfulness or get a massage or whatever makes you feel good, you'll be in a much better position to take care of your loved ones, because you'll be fit and healthy, both mentally and physically.

We've seen so many people in our therapy sessions who have given so much they've got nothing left and they feel continually exhausted or, worse, have become ill.

A good analogy to remind you of the importance of putting yourself first is thinking about the procedure when you take a flight on an airplane. The flight attendants always tell you that if the air pressure drops, you must put your own mask on before you help anyone else. So many people fall by the wayside in life because it's as though they're trying so hard to put masks on everyone else that they run out of air themselves. You have to administer oxygen to yourself before you can help and support anyone else.

Think of how many mothers run themselves into the ground looking after their family. But if they die early from illness as a result, leaving their children without a mother, their children will suffer a great deal more.

Society conditions us to believe that putting ourselves first occasionally is selfish, but the reality is that it's the complete opposite. You can't look after other people unless you can look after yourself.

Personally, we very rarely have to take time off work, or let people down due to illness, because we look after ourselves well. If we weren't in peak health we wouldn't be able to look after our patients or children anywhere near as well as we need to. Therefore, our diary, appointments, social life and business trips are organised around keeping fit and eating healthily, which is a priority for us.

Saying No

Doing things for your own happiness doesn't make you a bad person – you don't have to compromise your own needs for the sake of others. And honestly, they probably don't even want you to! If you keep putting everyone before yourself, you'll end up feeling frustrated, angry and resentful, and you can't be a great friend or parent if you're feeling that way.

We have a friend called Emma who always used to put everyone else's thoughts and feelings before her own, to the point where she didn't even stop and question what she was about to agree to. She would just say yes to something because it was her default setting. She thought that in order to be liked she had to keep everyone else happy all of the time, even if it meant making herself unhappy.

Not too long ago, Emma's friend Ailsa asked if she could come and stay for a night. Emma's spare room was filled with junk she needed to put in the loft. The bed sheets needed changing, and on top of that she had a friend coming for dinner the same night with whom she was keen to spend some one-on-one time. Without even thinking, she told Ailsa it was fine for her to stay and then spent the whole of that evening feeling angry about all the effort it was going to take to prepare the room for her guest. She was also cross that her dinner plans would be interrupted.

After giving it some thought, she texted Ailsa and said she was very sorry, but it wasn't convenient for her to stay after all, and she explained the situation. Ailsa texted back saying it wasn't a problem; she wasn't in the least bit offended.

Emma had wasted all of that time and energy getting worked up, upset and stressed when all she had to do was stop, think, put herself first and say no, which was perfectly understandable in view of the circumstances.

We tend to build things up so much and often think for other people. Emma had convinced herself that Ailsa would be cross if she said she couldn't stay. Her head was swimming with thoughts like: 'She'll be so offended. She'll think I don't like her. She won't like me as much. I'll really let her down.' How did Emma know how Ailsa would feel? Could she mind-read? Even if Ailsa had been a bit upset, she would soon get over it and, as it turned out, she didn't mind one bit.

The amazing thing is that once you regularly start to put yourself first, you'll find it easier and easier. The saying-yes default mode is a habit that can be broken.

Think about it: you've got certain friends who you know if they say no to a party invitation, then they mean no. However, you have other friends who, although they may initially say no, will cave in if you apply a little pressure. It's the ones who say no and mean it that we have the most respect for, and therefore we don't push our luck with them. Wouldn't you rather be the person people respect as opposed to the pushover?

Once Emma started being more honest with herself and saying no to things more often, she became a lot happier and more relaxed in her life overall. If someone was offended because she didn't fall into line with everything they expected from her, she understood that it was their issue. You can't keep everyone happy. Certainly not without making yourself unhappy.

Putting Yourself First

Saving yourself means making yourself a priority, the repercussions of which may not benefit only you, but also your friends, family and beyond, just like it did for J.K. Rowling.

J.K. Rowling is someone who took a long time to put herself first, but once she did, it paid off for her and her family in a huge way. She was a single mother and probably used to doing everything for other people and not giving herself much time and care. When she started writing the *Harry Potter* books, she used to sit in a café, pushing her pram with her foot to keep her baby soothed.

Some people may have looked at her and thought she was really selfish for writing for hours when she had a baby with her, but the reality was that she was saving herself and creating a future for her family.

If she had never allowed herself the space to start writing *Harry Potter*, her life, and that of her children, would have been very different. In fact, she may have ended up unhappy and resentful because she wasn't fulfilling her ambitions. By pursuing her dreams for that short period of time, she not only helped herself and her family, she has also helped an incredible number of other people through her charity work, while making millions of others incredibly happy through her fantastic storytelling.

Make a Decision

We had a patient called Ruth who had terrible depression when we met her. She had two daughters who were also miserable because their mother was always so unhappy at home. Ruth had been to her doctor to get medication and had been considering getting therapy for some time, but she kept thinking about how the money would be better spent on new coats or school shoes for her daughters.

One day, her husband told her she had to do something about her moods because their home life was unbearable, and their marriage was in danger of breaking down. Ruth started to see that she would lose everything if she didn't finally invest in herself.

We helped her address the origins of her issues and then to break through the negative pattern of depression she had fallen into. As part of our work with Ruth, we emphasised the importance of learning to look after herself. Ruth now has a great career, which involves her going into offices to coach people. As a result of her new-found independence and positive outlook, her marriage has improved dramatically. She and her husband have been able to move house, they've got nicer cars, they go on holiday and, in addition to the people she coaches, her whole family are much happier. She even sent us an email from a holiday in Australia, saying that she was finally experiencing the world. All this was a consequence of making a decision, taking action and then putting herself first.

Exercises

Give yourself a hug

Studies have shown that hugs have a positive effect on our bodies due to encouraging the release of feel-good endorphins. These endorphins promote healing, wellbeing, improved mood and even help reduce blood pressure. Here's a great technique to reap the benefits of a hug, even if you are alone.

1. **Close your eyes.**

2. **See an image of yourself in front of you in your mind's eye.**

3. **Make the image of yourself happy, confident, strong and healthy-looking.**

4. **Make that image big, bright, clear and colourful.**

5. **Grab that image as if you are giving it a hug.**

6. **Hold yourself close and notice how great that feels. Hold the feeling for a few seconds, allowing the sensation to expand, then open your eyes.**

Do this exercise at least twice each week and notice your inner power grow. Write a reminder for yourself in your diary, so you don't overlook yourself amid the hustle and bustle of daily life.

Why I deserve to be my priority

The following exercise will help you put yourself first and appreciate how your happiness is important not only to you, but also to your loved ones. Fill in the table opposite to help you see and appreciate why you deserve to be happy!

List all of those who love you (this can include pets, and also people who have loved you and passed away)	List reasons why this person loves you. What qualities do they see in you? What compliments have they given you, or why do they say they love you? 'I love you because . . .'	How would your happiness positively impact this person? How would it make them feel? How would it improve your relationship? How would it improve your life, moving forward?

(Table continued overleaf)

(Table continued)

List all of those who love you (this can include pets, and also people who have loved you and passed away)	List reasons why this person loves you. What qualities do they see in you? What compliments have they given you, or why do they say they love you? 'I love you because . . .'	How would your happiness positively impact this person? How would it make them feel? How would it improve your relationship? How would it improve your life, moving forward?

Affirmations

'I am the only person who will be with me twenty-four hours a day, seven days a week, for the rest of my life. I owe it to myself, and everyone I love, to put myself first.'

'Today and everyday, I choose to be confident.'

'I accept others for who they are and I accept me for who I will become.'

10

No One
Is Born Bad

Our tenth core schema – **no one is born bad** – creates a lot of debate when we share it at our workshops. But we stand by it, and we have seen how understanding this schema helps our clients. We aren't saying that people don't do bad things – but this core schema is about realising that sometimes people (even good people) can do bad things because of difficult circumstances they find themselves in.

Nature Versus Nurture

We like to use the 1983 comedy film *Trading Places* to illustrate this point. In the movie, Eddie Murphy plays a homeless conman, while Dan Aykroyd is a wealthy and successful commodities broker. When the two switch places as part of a debate over nature versus nurture, we see the contrast between socioeconomic statuses at opposite ends of the spectrum.

We see how Dan Aykroyd's character, who has lived a life of privilege, finds himself having to steal and cheat to survive. When placed in a terrible situation he becomes what is perceived to be a 'bad person'.

Meanwhile, Eddie Murphy's character also has his life turned around, becoming a better person as a result of being put into more plush surroundings and being given responsibility and respect, and therefore increased self-esteem and self-worth.

We believe the movie shows that no one is born 'good' or 'bad', but that our circumstances have a lot to do with how we experience life and the decisions we make as a result.

If someone ends up on the streets and the only way they could survive was by stealing food, they would steal food, no matter how good a person they were to start with. If you're in a life-or-death situation and you're being attacked, you might kill someone in self-defence, but this does not mean you're an evil person. This is human nature.

It works the other way as well, as depicted in the film. Someone can grow up in a terrible environment and end up doing bad things to survive, but it can sometimes take just one person to invest in them and show them that trust exists for them to turn their lives around.

A young black American woman was born into poverty in rural Mississippi to a teenage mother who left her for her first six years of life. She was so poor she wore dresses made from potato sacks. She was raped from the age of nine by numerous family members and then she ran away from home aged thirteen, becoming pregnant at the age of fourteen. Her son then died in infancy.

She went to live with the man she believed to be her father, who was strict but ensured she received a good education. She has two half-sisters: one was adopted, the other died of a drug overdose. And she had a half-brother who sadly died of AIDS at the age of twenty-nine.

Anyone looking at that life would expect this woman to have a very bleak future ahead. You may be surprised to learn that this is the life story of Oprah Winfrey. It's an amazing testimony to our ability to turn life around, despite facing the worst possible circumstances.

*

Of course, there are exceptions to every rule, and when we've talked about no one being born bad at our workshops people in the audience have opposed our belief. More than once, we've been asked how the likes of terrorists weren't born bad people.

Our view is that those people weren't born bad; they grew up in an environment where they were introduced to people who indoctrinated them with ideologies that are incomprehensible to us. Some extremists are conditioned to believe their actions honour their family. If you're brought up with that belief and it's all you know, you are unlikely ever to question it. Quite simply, you don't know any better. They're not bad people and they were not born with the intention of killing or hurting others; they have an incredible amount of fear brainwashed into them. It's a simple formula. We are all a product of our environment, and as such we simply copy behaviour.

If someone were to adopt a child from a violent extremist environment, and brought them up with kind, loving beliefs and values, they would likely be very different. We're all a product of our environment. Our upbringing can have a profound effect on our behaviours, beliefs and values. There is always a positive intent in everything we do, whether positive or negative, and this is based upon what we have been taught is acceptable or unacceptable.

Our path in life is so often dictated by our learned behaviour, and sadly people can grow up with good and bad examples to varying degrees. Obviously, not all learned behaviour leads to something as extreme as terrorism, but what we learn has an enduring impact on us, unless we challenge and then begin to change those behaviours by conditioning them with new evidence, information and thoughts.

Sure, there is a small percentage of people who don't want to change and who like behaving badly – there are exceptions to every rule. However, there are fewer of them than you think. If you took a 'bad' person and put them in good circumstances, the chances are you would see a positive change in them, just like in the film *Trading Places*. Likewise, if you put a good person in bad circumstances, the chances are they would change for the worse because they would have to fight to survive.

If, however, you believe that the world is full of bad people who make the world a terrible place, then the person who suffers from that belief is *you*.

As we said earlier in Chapter Three, if you believe people are bad, that's like mixing up a poison for someone else and drinking it yourself, because you're the one who's going to feel frightened, sick and angry. Those negative feelings won't affect the people you see as 'bad', but they will make you unhappy, sad and bitter.

If you do perceive that someone has a negative effect on you through their actions, you have a choice as to whether or not you want to interact with that person. You need to take a step back and consider how other people can affect the way you feel, especially if you are trying to change elements of your life in order to get a more positive outcome in the long term.

Fleas

There is a saying – 'If you lie down with dogs, you will get up with fleas.' When our cats Feeniks, Banksy, Scooter, Monkey and Buddy Elf get fleas and ticks, we give them a treatment and within forty-eight hours they are tick- and flea-free. The treatment lasts two months, so if they kept away from fleas and ticks, they would never need another application again. However, they like going over to the farm near our house and playing with the farm cats, all of which have fleas, so guess what? Yes, as soon as the treatment wears off they get fleas and ticks again, and subsequently need treating again.

A similar thing happens with the people we spend time with. You can work on yourself time and time again and take massive steps forward, but if you still surround yourself with negative people who are determined to pull you back, it's equivalent to playing with a cat with fleas. Make no mistake, negative people will contaminate you and your world, therefore it's vital that you take a close look at your social circles. If you keep going back to the same circles hoping for a different outcome, the likelihood is that unless they've changed (never mind you), you'll be flea-ridden again before you know it.

Changes

It's also important to make you aware that when you take responsibility for your life and start the process of change, not everyone may love the in-control, positive, happy new you straight away. Often people don't like to see their friends or family changing because they're comfortable with who they perceive them to be. This is especially the case if the changes affect them in ways that they're not happy with.

For example, if a brother is used to being able to push his sister around and manipulate her into doing what he wants, and then all of a sudden that sister is standing up for herself, the brother won't like it one little bit. Why should he have to go and visit their sick grandma when she can do it? She always used to, so what's the problem now? Why should he have to buy a birthday present for their dad when she can get it while she's buying hers? The brother's schema may be that the sister will always do what he wants, so he is less than happy when that's challenged.

On top of that, the people around you may even be jealous, because they don't feel like they're moving on with their lives or making positive changes in the same way you are.

It may be that you can no longer be around those who don't have your best interests at heart, at least until they've accepted that the new you isn't going to magically morph back into the passive person you were before.

The happier and more positive you feel, the more you'll notice who is good for you and who isn't. Part of saving yourself is moving away from people who contaminate you, in whatever negative form that takes.

Just consider, if you have five friends who smoke, then you are likely to smoke too, just as if you have five friends who are broke or unhappy, then you are more likely to be the sixth. When you consider this, you realise how important it is to surround yourself with people who are not like you but are like who you want to be! If you don't have any of those people in your life, then you need to start looking for them.

Supporters, Igniters, Draggers

We would like you to consider placing the people in your life into three categories – supporters, igniters and draggers. (See the exercise on page 199 to help you do this once you have read the definitions.)

Supporters

Supporters are friends and family who do exactly that: support you no matter what. Whatever you do, right or wrong, they are always there for you and are never judgemental about your actions. They may question what you do, but always from a place of wanting to understand and uplift.

Igniters

Igniters are rare and hard to find, but when you find them they are wonderful. They're the people who make you feel like you are amazing and can do anything. They encourage you, push you forward and always want the best for you. They may make you laugh till your sides ache and are a complete and utter joy to be around. Your phone rings and, no matter what you are doing, if you see an igniter's name flashing up on the screen, you will always answer.

Draggers

Lastly, there are draggers; these are the people who bring you down. The phone test above works the opposite way for draggers – your mobile phone rings, you go to pick it up, but when you see the name of the caller on your phone you slump and get that 'oh no' feeling. In fact, not only do you often not take the call, but you have to build up the energy to call them back. This should instantly tell you that the person in question isn't good for you. They zap positive energy and self-belief out of you. They can literally be like the Dementors in *Harry Potter*.

No matter how many times we tell you all of the simple but amazing ways you can make your life better, if you still hang around with draggers who breed negativity, they will keep pulling you back.

This schema is not actually about negative people at all. It's about you, and allowing yourself to let go of the anger or resentment you may have towards those who have wronged you. The aim is to encourage you to consider the actions of others more before passing judgement on them, which in turn will make your world a less constricted and brighter place.

Exercises

We accept that this core schema can be the toughest and most challenging to take onboard. We are sure there will have been people in your life that have been unkind or insulting to you or made you feel ashamed, embarrassed, humiliated, inadequate, unattractive, vulnerable or worthless.

We hope that having read this much of our book, you now realise that no one has the right to make you feel bad in any way. We also hope you can understand that those upsetting actions, while unacceptable, were not personal to you, but most likely the unintentional result of someone's own insecurities or difficult circumstances. We aren't suggesting you have to forgive bad behaviour, but we are suggesting that you let go of any hurtful words and actions directed towards you, to free yourself.

Carrying the emotional pain of someone else's vitriol is like choosing to keep them in your life and allowing them to influence you each day. They will almost certainly be oblivious to any hatred or anger you continue to harbour against them, therefore the only person continuing to suffer is you, and you deserve better.

Today is the day to cut those emotional ties with the negative people in your life.

Altering the effects of unkindness

The following exercise will help you work on changing your perception of and emotions towards negative people.

List anyone who has hurt you or whose unkindness still affects you	Why might they have been unkind? What circumstances might have created their behaviour and attitude?	What positive can you take from what happened between you and this person?
Example: School bully (use their name here)	Examples: Bad home life; low self-esteem; being bullied; not achieving what they wanted in life; lacking intelligence, etc.	Examples: I'm stronger because of them; I'm more empathetic; I can give others first-hand advice; I know they were envious, which means I had something to envy, etc.

(Table continued overleaf)

(Table continued)

List anyone who has hurt you or whose unkindness still affects you	Why might they have been unkind? What circumstances might have created their behaviour and attitude?	What positive can you take from what happened between you and this person?

Take the mobile phone test

Look through your list of contacts in your mobile phone and imagine how you would feel if each person were to call you. If you have any shred of reluctance, dread or negativity at the sight of their name, you can define that person as a dragger (see page 195) and make a decision to distance yourself from them, or at least keep them at arm's length.

We understand that draggers are more often than not family members or work colleagues, so if you can't distance yourself then you must either change how you deal with them (i.e. always be pleasant and upbeat to counter their negativity) or change your perception of them. For example, why not secretly give them a nickname or liken them to a character from television or film to help elevate your mood when you're around them? Do not share this with them, though! It's just an internal trick to help you manage their negativity without getting sucked in.

Conversely, look at the people who you would always be happy to speak to, those whose voices makes you feel immediately better, and make a point of speaking to them more often. They are supporters or, even better, igniters (see page 195), and they are positive, not negative, influences on your life.

Affirmation

> *'Bad people aren't born that way; they're victims themselves, created by bad circumstances and beliefs. I will actively seek out igniters and avoid draggers.'*

11

You've Got To Give To Receive

Our eleventh schema – **you've got to give to receive** – is one that we initially found quite confusing ourselves. The concept seems counterintuitive. We couldn't understand how giving your money away could generate more. Maybe that's because we initially thought of the schema in terms of material possessions. Then one day the reality of this statement hit Nik, and he's going to tell this story.

NIK

I would often hear our son Hunter tell Eva that he loved her, but he never told me the same. Every night when Hunter went to bed, Eva would tell him she loved him, and he would respond that he loved her too.

One day I asked him, 'Do you love your dad?' He replied, 'Of course I do.' Yet he still did not volunteer those three very special words 'I love you'.

When considering this I realised that I actually never told Hunter I loved him. I wondered why that was and realised my dad never told me he loved me, nor me him. My dad absolutely did love me – he showed me his love constantly, so it sort of went without saying. But I realised that I had copied that behaviour with Hunter.

I now wanted something different from my father–son relationship so, as change starts with change, I started telling Hunter every night that I loved him. After two weeks, very randomly as we were walking along, he took my hand and said, 'I love you, Dad.' My heart melted, and I will never forget that day. That change continued: every day I still tell him I love him and he tells me too.

However, this would never have happened if I hadn't changed the way I had been with Hunter. It's amazing how quickly things can turn around. And the change started with me, not him.

The Gift of a Compliment

It's incredible how giving to charity or doing kind things for people comes back to you. Even just giving someone a smile in the street can make a massive difference. Think how good you feel when someone smiles or says hello to you for no reason. You can be walking down a busy street and feeling grumpy about the fact that there are so many people around. Then, if you bump into someone and they smile or make a light-hearted comment about how crowded it is or give you a simple compliment like, 'I love your coat,' it can put a little spring in your step.

You most definitely get back what you put out into the world. You can very easily change someone's day with just a kind word or a compliment.

We love compliments, which benefit the giver as much as the receiver. If you have the mindset that whenever you see someone you're going to find something positive to compliment them on, your kind words can stay with them for days. Furthermore, you will feel great for making someone happy, and that feeling really is priceless. You may also find that they even compliment you back, so it's a huge win-win situation! Let's face it, who doesn't love that? Just think how many times in the day you admire someone's hair or their dress, their coat, their shoes. Having that lovely thought and not telling them is like having a gift for someone and withholding it. If you have a nice thought about someone, tell them.

Just as compliments can uplift us, so throwaway comments can bring us down, so be careful what you say in unguarded moments. When children get told they'll never amount to anything by intolerant, fed-up teachers they can soak up those harsh words and may grow up thinking they're always going to be a failure. That ill-thought-out remark can sink into the unconscious and create a schema that could negatively impact that child's life forevermore.

This is where we go back to the third schema of accepting responsibility (see Chapter Three). Only you can challenge and change those thoughts and realise that they are wrong.

What we would like you to consider is that the world is like a mirror, so everything you put out will come back to you, eventually.

Whatever people think about Simon Cowell, he gives and receives like a pro. Some people think he's a money-making machine or they're jealous of his success, but he's given a lot of people a lot of incredible opportunities they would never have had before. Some of the people who have appeared on his shows would never have got the chance to leap into the limelight or get a record deal otherwise. Whether you agree with the way he works or not, it's hard not to feel inspired by him on some level. If there's one man who believes in himself and knows that he'll have an even more successful future, it's Simon Cowell.

If we're looking at the schema of giving to receive from a material or monetary point of view, the example we like to share relates to when we first set up our business. We knew we wanted to help people and, at first, we saw a lot of clients for free. As a result, they recommended us to people, who then came along and paid us for therapy, and in those earlier years when we were building our business and our reputation, we also offered a money-back guarantee.

We still treat people for free to this day. Each month we ask our office to find someone in the locality, among the thousands of emails we receive, who has a phobia, whom we can cure for free. It's always so incredibly rewarding. Similarly, if we see someone in the street who is suffering, we will always offer to help if we have the time to stop. The payback is priceless. We love seeing people happy, so we will always do what we can to make that happen if we are able.

Exercise

Smile, give compliments, share nice thoughts, make an effort to speak to people at work you'd normally ignore and compliment them on their contribution.

Tell your partner, children, family and friends you love them. Call an old aunt to see how she is. Donate something to the local charity shop. Do as many things as you can to make your world a nicer place and then you will reap the emotional rewards.

Unconscious habits are created from conscious actions, therefore a great way to make this happen is to keep a kindness diary.

Note in the table opposite, or in your daily diary if you use one, one kind action each day for the next four weeks. This can be anything from a nice gesture to sharing a kind word, giving someone a compliment or presenting someone with a material gift or even a hug.

My kindness diary

WEEK 1	Act of kindness
Monday	
Tuesday	
Wednesday	
Thursday	
Friday	
Saturday	
Sunday	

WEEK 2	Act of kindness
Monday	
Tuesday	
Wednesday	
Thursday	
Friday	
Saturday	
Sunday	

WEEK 3	Act of kindness
Monday	
Tuesday	
Wednesday	
Thursday	
Friday	
Saturday	
Sunday	

WEEK 4	Act of kindness
Monday	
Tuesday	
Wednesday	
Thursday	
Friday	
Saturday	
Sunday	

Affirmations

'The world is a mirror. What I put out will reflect back at me.'

'I will put out love, kindness, gratitude and success.'

'I live a perfect day by helping someone who will never be able to repay me.'

'The greatest differences I will make to the world are the ones I don't see.'

12

You Become What You Think About

Our final core schema is that **you become what you think about**. This schema basically sums up all of the others in one. We are our thoughts, and our thoughts dictate our actions. So doesn't it make sense that we should make our thoughts as positive and optimistic as possible?

If you believe you'll never amount to anything, the chances are you won't. American industrialist Henry Ford, founder of the Ford Motor Company, supposedly said, 'Whether you think you can or think you can't – you're right.' If you think you're the ugly one, you may as well be. That may sound harsh, but it's true. Who will cheerlead for you if you won't cheerlead for yourself first?

At the opposite end of the spectrum, there are some people who may not be that talented or good-looking but think they're better than everyone else, hence developing a superiority complex. Being delusional about your abilities isn't necessarily the best way to be, but it's better than always telling yourself you're no good. At least if you think you're incredible, you won't care what other people say about you, thus providing a cast-iron emotional shield.

The real trick is to find the middle ground: to be happy with yourself without being arrogant. There is definitely a very fine line between self-belief and arrogance!

Happiness from Within

Lucy is thirty-seven, pretty and a statuesque size sixteen. She knows she's never going to be a size eight, but she wakes up every day happy – because she is happy with herself.

As she said to us: 'People may not walk into a room and think I'm the thinnest or the prettiest girl in there, but as soon as I start a conversation with someone I win them over because I'm fun to be around. I don't carry around a "Poor me, I'm not skinny" attitude; I embrace what I've got, and as a result I'm great company. I've never found it difficult to attract men and have often found myself laughing the night away with the most attractive man at a party, while a modelesque girl stands in the corner on her own, pouting miserably. Friends who I deem to be beautiful and far better-looking than me ask me for lessons in pulling. It's hilarious.'

She went on to say, 'I don't hanker to be anything other than what I am. I learned a long time ago that I just want to be the best me I can be, and that means embracing my flaws as well as my attributes and my dark side as well as my light.' Lucy is a perfect example of how our thoughts create our world.

If you change your thoughts and your actions, you can totally change your life. The process of using our twelve core schemas is all about changing your thought patterns. If you say you won't ever trust anyone again, you won't let anyone into your world. But if you tell yourself you do trust people, you'll be letting in the good ones. Yes, there may well be a dodgy few here and there, but part of this book, as we've mentioned earlier, is to appreciate that you have a choice as to who you have in your life.

There's a proverb that says, 'Prepare for the worst, but hope for the best.' That's not telling you to be negative, it's just saying that some bad things may happen and to be aware of that, but you should always hope for the best, because – let's be honest here – that's what you deserve.

Really think about the way you say things – to yourself and others – and notice the effect certain words have on you. If you are slightly annoyed about something but tell your friend that you're 'absolutely furious', you will end up feeling that level of anger. Think about what happens when someone tells you that you look tired. You immediately feel tired, don't you? If you're bunking off work when you're actually fine, you often end up feeling ill because on a subconscious level you're telling yourself you are.

Thoughts Create Feelings

Thoughts and emotions create physical symptoms in the same way they create our future through action, which is why it's so important to be aware of how you're feeling when you say things to yourself. The words you say to yourself are more powerful than the words you say to others. You can totally change a situation by changing your emotional reaction to it. For instance, if someone purposely steals the last car parking space right from under your nose, you can either get so cross you feel your heart pounding and the beginnings of a headache, or you can take a deep breath and think how awful it must be to be the kind of person who would do something so mean. Who's the winner then?

It's much the same with worry. Worry is nothing more than a down payment on a loan that you very rarely, if ever, will take out.

Our friend Simon lives in a flat in London. He's been there for five years and the flat below him has been empty the entire time. He's discovered that actually it's quite nice without neighbours, as he can make noise and no one complains.

However, his mum is constantly worrying that squatters are going to move in, and every time she speaks to Simon she reminds him that it will be harder for him to sell his flat if the downstairs one is an empty mess. Simon's reply is, 'I'm not planning on moving for a while, Mum, so why worry about something I don't need to be concerned with? The owner could choose to do it up tomorrow and everything will be fine. If he doesn't, I'll cross that bridge when I come to it, otherwise it's wasted energy.'

There is no point in Simon spending the next few years getting worked up and stressed about something that he can't do anything about. In fact, the constant nagging from his mum was more stressful than the problem itself, before he politely asked her to stop talking about it!

The best example we can possibly give of thoughts creating feelings is that of a family member. She has always been a really outgoing woman with wild platinum-blonde hair, a full face of make-up and a great sense of humour. She always looked after herself well and was the life and soul of every party.

One day she got a cough that wouldn't go away and, following some tests, she was diagnosed with lung cancer. Doctors told her that, coupled with her advancing age, it was too aggressive for them to do anything about, so they told her to go off and enjoy the remainder of her life.

Overnight she became what she thought she was: a woman who was dying of cancer. She stopped going out and putting on make-up, and she lost her appetite, and therefore lost a lot of weight. She had no energy and her family felt like they were watching her die right in front of their eyes.

Two months later, she got a phone call asking her to go to the hospital urgently. When she saw the doctor he turned to her and said, 'I'm so, so sorry. We mixed up your records with someone else's and you actually had pleurisy – you don't have cancer.'

Soon she transformed from a frail, dying, weak cancer sufferer back to her old fun-loving, flamboyant self, with her make-up back on, chatting and laughing with friends and loving life. Had she not been told that she didn't have cancer, who's to say she wouldn't have died anyway, because she had effectively given up on life? The minute she knew she wasn't dying, she started living again. The change in her was nothing short of incredible.

You're as Old as You Believe You Are

One of our friends, Alan, was telling us about his grandmother, who always looked amazing for her age. However, the minute she turned sixty, she seemed to age overnight. To her, sixty was 'old age', and she was constantly churning out the mantra, 'Well, of course I can't do that, I'm sixty now, you know.'

Alan said that not only did he see an emotional change in his grandma in the years that followed that milestone birthday, but physically she went from looking incredible and youthful to turning into a little old lady. It was as if turning sixty had given her an excuse to give up on life and have everyone running around after her, feeling sorry for her. What a waste of those years!

The bottom line is, we believe what we're told. If you look at everything from voodoo to witchcraft, even though there is no scientific proof whatsoever that these mystical practices are effective, many, many people are convinced that they work. If you told someone who believes in voodoo that you'd put a spell on them and they were going to get very ill as a result, the likelihood is that they would. This would not be the result of any actual spell, but of the suggestion, the fear and the fact that their belief is so strong. It's also the case that if someone we have total faith in tells us something we want to believe in, we will go out of our way to make it happen, whether consciously or unconsciously.

At the moment, tarot is very popular, and many people are convinced that tarot readers can predict their future. While tarot can be a bit of fun, it's important to remember that we are all masters of our own destiny and we can make decisions and take action to entirely alter our current path in life, no matter what the cards 'predict'.

Believing in a prediction about your future is just another form of planning your life. If you believe without question that what someone is telling you is true, you're focusing all of your energy on that prediction. As we know, that's incredibly powerful because it activates the brain's reticular activating system, which, as we discussed earlier (see pages 139–43), works just like a radar or putting a destination into the satellite-navigation system in your car. Just as the affirmation on page 110 says, every acorn has an oak tree within it. Just like the oak tree, if you want to grow to your full potential, you have to start thinking like an oak and not an acorn; you have to start thinking like the person you want to become, not the person you currently are.

I Am What I Say I Am

Let's look at what kinds of 'I am' statements come out of your mouth, as these can hugely affect your life and how you behave. So, what do you say about yourself? For so many people that internal voice is negative: I am a failure, I am never any good, I am useless, I am difficult, I am undisciplined, I am unattractive, I am always making mistakes, I am depressed.

No one would approach someone in the street and say those terrible things to their face, and yet remarkably we often have no problem saying those things to ourselves.

We'd urge you never to say negative things about yourself, just as you'd never say them to anyone else. Negative thoughts mean a negative future. Let's be honest, here: you may have enough challenges in life already, without you being against yourself too. So if you change your 'I am' statements into positive ones, you can take your life to a whole new level.

Consider using phrases such as: I am grateful, I am talented, I am victorious, I am blessed, I am strong, I am amazing, I am attractive, I am successful, I am free, I am kind, I am confident.

Always make sure that you have the right 'I ams' coming out of your mouth. The new 'I ams' may not feel true for you right now, but you have to read them and say them out loud as if they already were. Keep doing this: say them out loud and be proud, and one day you will suddenly wake up and feel amazing and realise exactly just how wonderful you are.

If it's hard to say these phrases, then you can try saying 'I am becoming . . .' first. For example: I am becoming successful, I am becoming healthy, I am becoming confident. This can help you get to a point where you can use 'I am' on its own.

LEWIS HAMILTON

Our final incredible example of becoming what you think about is a story of a young boy who walked up to McLaren Formula 1 team boss Ron Dennis, said, 'Hi, I'm Lewis Hamilton. I won the British Championship [karting cadet class] and one day I want to be racing your cars.' Ron told Lewis to call him in nine years' time and they'd sort something out.

In reality, it took only a few years until Lewis Hamilton was officially signed to the McLaren Driver Development Programme (now the McLaren Young Driver Programme), becoming the youngest driver at that time to have ever been contracted by an F1 team.

Lewis's dream started after receiving a radio-controlled car from his dad when he was six years of age; he became obsessed with racing. His father bought him his first go-kart as a Christmas present and told him that he would support his racing career as long as he worked hard at school.

It didn't take Lewis long to start winning, and he won his first British go-karting championship at the age of eight. Aged twenty-two, Lewis started driving F1 for McLaren. Remarkably, at the end of his debut season Lewis ended up only one point behind that year's drivers' champion, the seasoned professional Kimi Räikkönen. In addition to coming second in his debut season, Lewis also recorded nine consecutive podium finishes – more than any other rookie in F1 history.

The following season, in 2008, Lewis clinched the F1 World Championship, becoming the youngest driver to win the title. He was also the first British driver to win the World Championship since Damon Hill, who triumphed in 1996.

Lewis's story continues to be more and more incredible, as he has become the best British F1 driver in history, equalling Michael Schumacher's record of seven World Championship titles.

With Lewis continuing to race, who knows what may happen? And how exciting that he could even surpass the superlative Michael Schumacher. Thankfully, Lewis's dad believed and supported the dreams of that six-year-old boy who became exactly what he thought about.

You don't need to go to a tarot reader to predict your future – you can predict it by choosing what you want and creating it yourself.

Exercises

The perfect character

Imagine that you are writing a movie script and you are creating the perfect character that you want and need to be to fulfil your dreams.

Write a list of your perfect character's mannerisms and attitudes and, just like a movie role, rehearse and then perform them, first in your mind, then alone to a mirror and then in real-life situations.

Practice makes perfect, and you will soon be able to adopt these new, empowering behaviours in everyday life. At first this will require conscious effort; however, with practice, it will become habitual and effortless.

....

....

....

....

....

....

....

....

I am . . .

Make a list of a minimum of ten positive 'I am' or 'I am becoming . . .' phrases and read them often throughout the day, saying them out loud and meditating on them.

1. I am ....

2. I am ....

3. I am ....

4. I am ....

5. I am ....

6. I am ....

7. I am ....

8. I am ....

9. I am ....

10. I am ....

Gratitude list

As you know from Chapter Three, to be happy we have to **accept responsibility** and take measures to create happiness. Our brain's primary function is to keep us safe, rather than make us happy, and so we have to consciously provide the ingredients to create happiness in our lives.

Creating a gratitude list to read every morning will help to elevate your mood. Being aware of the things you are grateful for sets you up for a better day, even if challenging things happen later. And you begin to train your brain to look out for things to be grateful for in your daily life.

We would now like you to write that gratitude list. This should include things you have experienced, seen or visited and times you have laughed uncontrollably, felt love or been in love, as well as family, friends, your sight, your abilities, the fact that you woke up, that you have a home, car, job, education, etc. These are just examples to consider; this is your list, so document everything and anything you are grateful for.

I AM GRATEFUL FOR . . .

....

....

....

....

....

....

....

....

....

(List continued overleaf)

....

....

....

....

....

....

....

....

WOW list

You can also take steps to create a better night's sleep and a more positive frame of mind for morning by creating a WOW list to read every night to complement your gratitude list.

Your WOW list can include everything you've tried, seen or experienced that you were thrilled by, proud of, pleasantly surprised by or elated about. You can add things such as a show you saw that was WOW, a gesture, compliment or gift someone gave you that was WOW, a holiday that was WOW, a proposal that was WOW, a meal or night out that was WOW. Basically, a list of what is WOW about you!

MY WOW LIST

....

....

....

....

....

....

....

....

....

....

....

....

....

....

....

Gratitude letter

Finally, we would like you to think of someone who you are grateful for, who you admire or who has shown you great kindness. This could be a partner, parent, friend, former school teacher, work colleague or neighbour.

We would like you to write a letter to the person below:

Dear ....

I just want you to know that I think you are . . .

....

....

....

....

....

....

Because . . .

....

....

....

....

....

....

....

I admire you and am grateful to you because . . .

....

....

....

....

....

....

....

Quite often, we think things but don't say them, and I just
wanted you to know how much I care about you, value you
and admire you, and I am aware that I wouldn't be where
I am today if it wasn't for you.

Much love ....

Now you have written this letter, we would like you to call
this person and say:

'Hi ....

'It's ....

'I just wanted to call you as I am taking part in the
Speakmans' Upgrade Your Life programme and part of this
upgrade involves being aware of the things around me that
I am grateful for, and the people who have had a positive
impact on me in my life. I have been asked to write a letter
to that person, and I would like you to please listen to what
I have written.'   .

> ### *READ YOUR LETTER ABOVE TO THEM*

After the call, note below how this exercise has positively
impacted on you:

....

....

....

....

....

....

....

....

....

....

Now note how this exercise has positively impacted on the person you called:

....

....

....

....

....

....

....

....

....

....

You should notice that both you and the recipient of your call felt happier and grateful for one another after completing this exercise – it might even bring you even closer. Furthermore, this exercise has helped you action two of our core schemas: **you've got to give to receive** (see Chapter Eleven) and **you become what you think about** (see Chapter Twelve).

WELL DONE!

Affirmations

'Literally anything is possible. I can be whatever or whoever I choose to be.'

'There is no room in my life for negativity.'

'My ideas and thoughts are good enough; I do not need to seek validation from others.'

'I love and accept myself.'

Conclusion:
It's Time
to Take Action

We have now shared with you the twelve core schemas that have helped us to completely transform our lives as well as the lives of so many others over the years.

Do these core schemas work?

Absolutely, yes!

But *only if you do!*

You are the best project you will ever work on and, as we said earlier, the harder you work, the luckier you will get. So please, please, don't just put this book down and expect your life to change because you've read our words.

You now have the tools and also some amazing evidential examples of how some people, perhaps just like you, have turned their lives around.

Now it's your turn to transform your life.

We really, really want you to upgrade your life, and with the schemas and exercises in this book we know that you can. We cannot, however, take responsibility for your life for you. Believe us, if we could, we would, as we really just want the very best for you. So please, make the choice to transform your life and complete the exercises in this book and put the twelve core schemas into action, as you really do deserve the upgraded version of you.

We've never tried to impress anyone with what we have personally achieved, but we always try to impress upon people that, just like us, they can have all the success and happiness they want if they are prepared to create it. That's exactly why we are so keen to spread the word to as many people as we can.

If you look back to where we started out compared to where we are now, you can clearly see that we've taken this journey to upgrade our lives ourselves. We're not asking you to do anything that we, or thousands of others, haven't already done before.

We've had our challenges – we still do, as no one is immune to them – but nothing was handed to us on a plate; we simply set our goals, made our life plans and followed them with the help of the tools we have shared with you here.

Not only did we put our method to the test on ourselves, but we've also got thousands of examples of people for whom our twelve core schemas have worked. The core schemas are the key that will open a new and exciting future for you.

We've given you the plan, now all you need to do is take action, by reminding yourself frequently of the steps, exercises and mindset that will make your world a bigger, brighter and better place to be in.

Here's a reminder of your new twelve core schemas:

1. **There is no one reality.**

2. **Disregard the doubters.**

3. **Accept responsibility.**

4. **Anything is possible.**

5. **Failure only exists when you quit.**

6. **It's never too late.**

7. **Plan your life.**

8. **You are what you eat.**

9. **Save yourself before you save the world.**

10. **No one is born bad.**

11. **You've got to give to receive.**

12. **You become what you think about.**

We understand that you may not even want to adopt all twelve schemas at once, especially if you don't agree with them 100 per cent at this moment in time. Or you may choose to action one each month to entirely transform yourself over the coming year. What we can be sure of is that if you accept them and continually practise them, they will change your life. They changed ours and they continue to do so, and we want the same for you.

But now it is up to you.

This could be one of the first big choices you make entirely for yourself, by yourself. The first of many. Start now, not tomorrow. You see, once you start, there's a chain reaction that motivates you to keep going. And if you find that you need some more motivation plus a greater understanding of our core schemas, please do join us at one of our live workshops where we give many more examples of our core schemas.

There is no excuse big enough or good enough to deprive you of the amazing life that you deserve. You now need to tap into your self-discipline, which, as the word 'self' implies, comes 100 per cent from you. This will help you adopt the core schemas we have shared, and when you do that, the success will come.

We would like to take the opportunity to wish you the most fantastic life ahead, filled with an abundance of happiness, success and health. And if you would like to share your successes and transformations with us, we would love to hear from you @TheSpeakmans on Facebook, Twitter, Instagram and TikTok.

We know you can become whoever and whatever you wish, and that your future can be amazing if you implement our twelve core schemas in your life, follow the exercises suggested and take steps each day to make it so.

We believe in you!

Sending you all our love and encouragement,

Nik & Eva Speakman x

References

1   Laure Schnabel, Emmanuelle Kesse-Guyot, Benjamin Allès, et al, 'Association Between Ultraprocessed Food Consumption and Risk of Mortality Among Middle-aged Adults in France', *JAMA Internal Medicine* (February 2019), 179(4): 490–8, JAMA Network. https://jamanetwork.com/journals/jamainternalmedicine/article-abstract/2723626?utm_campaign=articlePDF&utm_medium=articlePDFlink&utm_source=articlePDF&utm_content=jamainternmed.2018.7289

2   Dinyadarshini Johnson, Sivakumar Thurairajasingam, Vengadesh Letchumanan, Kok-Gan Chan and Learn-Han Lee, 'Exploring the Role and Potential of Probiotics in the Field of Mental Health: Major Depressive Disorder', *Nutrients* (May 2021), 13(5): 1728. https://www.ncbi.nlm.nih.gov/pmc/articles/PMC8161395/

3   https://www.medicalnewstoday.com/articles/292693

4   'Did this grandfather, 78, really beat "incurable" cancer just by changing his diet?' *Daily Mail Online* (September 2012). https://www.dailymail.co.uk/health/article-2204080/Grandfather-incurable-cancer-given-clear-swapping-red-meat-dairy-products-10-fruit-veg-day.html

Acknowledgements

Our thanks to everyone who has supported and believed in us, even before we proved publicly that the perceived impossible is possible. Your support, belief, loyalty and friendship fuel our determination to share our message of hope and healing, regardless of people's past, pessimistic diagnoses or unjustified labels. After all, 'it's not what is wrong with you, it is what happened to you.'

We would like to acknowledge the most profound statements that have positively impacted and changed our lives for the better:

'Great spirits have always encountered violent opposition from mediocre minds.' **Einstein**

'There is nothing either good or bad, but thinking makes it so.' **Shakespeare**

'Whether you think you can or think you can't – you're right.' **Henry Ford**

'Whatever the mind can conceive and believe, it can achieve.' **Napoleon Hill**

'There is always a way and everything can be fixed.' **Frank Speakman** (Nik's dad)

About the Authors

Nik and Eva Speakman have studied and worked together since 1992, and have studied human behaviour and psychology for almost seven decades between them. They both share an uncontainable passion to offer hope and help people lead happier and less inhibited lives.

The Speakmans believe all suffering stems from trauma and that 'it's not what's wrong with you, it's what happened to you.'

Through studying the research of revolutionary psychologists such as John Watson, Jean Piaget, Albert Bandura, Lev Vygotsky and B. F. Skinner, Nik and Eva acquired an intellectual curiosity for behaviourism and behavioural conditioning. After many remarkable breakthroughs, their studies transformed into the creation of their own behavioural change therapy, known as Schema Conditioning Psychotherapy®.

Their work with trauma victims and their related symptoms, such as PTSD, CPTSD, dissociation disorder and depersonalisation, led to the creation of further exceptional trauma-based therapies, Visual Schema Displacement Therapy (VSDT)® and Visual Schema Detachment & Restructuring (VSDR)®.

Qualifications from the creation of their therapies have seen the Speakmans train psychology professors, doctors and Masters students at universities in both Amsterdam and Utrecht. In 2015, this training resulted in the first scientific studies being conducted into the workings of their therapy; the first two study papers highlighting their therapies' remarkable efficacy was published in the *Journal of Behaviour Therapy and Experimental Psychiatry* in June 2019. The third study, with a significantly larger set of participants, was published in the *European Journal of Psychotraumatology* in April 2021. A fourth scientific study (with hospital patients) is currently underway and will be completed by the end of 2022.

As well as members of the public, the couple work with and have treated many high-profile clients around the world, and they have had countless successes.

Nik and Eva help people through as many mediums as they can – including live workshops, tours, books, podcasts, radio, television, social media and YouTube. At the heart of all of the Speakmans' plans lies a relentless mission to offer hope to as many people as possible, to assist them in overcoming their issues and to help them improve the quality of their lives.

Notes

....

....

....

....

....

....

....

....

....

....

....

....

....

....